THE
HORSE CURE

TRUE STORIES

Remarkable Horses Bringing
Miraculous Change to Humankind

Michelle Holling-Brooks
Photographs by AJ Morey

TRAFALGAR SQUARE
North Pomfret, Vermont

First published in 2019 by
Trafalgar Square Books
North Pomfret, Vermont 05053

Trafalgar Square Books encourages the use of approved safety helmets in all equestrian sports and activities.

Library of Congress Cataloging-in-Publication Data
Names: Holling-Brooks, Michelle (Michelle Sheree), 1977- author.
Title: The horse cure : true stories: remarkable horses bringing miraculous change to humankind / Michelle Holling-Brooks ; photos by AJ (Ann-Janine) Morey.
Description: North Pomfret, Vertmont : Trafalgar Square Books, 2019. |
  Includes bibliographical references.
Identifiers: LCCN 2018052327 | ISBN 9781570769368 (pbk.)
Subjects: LCSH: Horsemanship--Therapeutic use. | Human-animal relationships.
Classification: LCC RM931.H6 H65 2019 | DDC 615.8/51581--dc23
LC record available at https://lccn.loc.gov/2018052327

Photographs by AJ Morey
Book design by Lauryl Eddlemon
Cover design by RM Didier
Index by Michelle Guiliano, LinebyLineIndexing.com
Typefaces: Minion, Myriad
Printed in the United States of America
10 9 8 7 6 5 4 3 2 1

*To all the horses that are willing
to partner with us for healing—
we thank you.*

CONTENTS

PREFACE

Why Horses?

Horses have been a huge part of my life since the young age of six. Working with horses started as a recreational sport for me. I rode and my sister played soccer. Little did my parents know that their decision to sign me up for the local parks and recreation riding program would turn into a lifelong passion and eventually evolve into my current mission of helping people find healing.

When I was 13 years old my life was turned upside down due to a severe illness. Horses provided a lifeline to find my footing again. They taught me it was okay to trust and be open to love. They taught me I was not broken, a victim, or "less than" because I had trauma in my life. Horses gave so much to me, I knew that working with them in partnership in order to assist other humans was my life's purpose. Starting in 2000 I began to work as a certified professional in the Equine-Assisted Activities and Therapies (EAAT) field. And in 2008 I founded Unbridled Change™, a full-time, non-profit organization providing mental health programs that offer a safe space for all beings (humans and horses) to heal and thrive.

For me, this book is over 27 years in the making. My hope for this project is that you, the reader, will gain a rare glimpse into what Equine-Partnered Psychotherapy and Coaching™ (EPPC) sessions feel and look like. I want to help you experience, through the power of stories, what a partnership with horses can co-create in the scope of healing the human soul. Whether you are new to the field of equine activities and therapies, a seasoned practitioner, or a person looking for recovery, I hope you find that this book opens a gateway to the power of horses as a partner on that journey.

How to Read This Book

Maybe you are wondering, why horses? What makes a horse such an amazing partner? Why are we drawn to partnering human healing and growth with horses as a key component in treatment? By the end of this book, my hope is that, like our clients at Unbridled Change, you will begin to find your own answers to those questions. While I can totally "geek out" on research, explanation, and teaching the how's and why's, that's not how I start with clients. I don't really dive into all the information, science, and background for this model of therapy. Instead, I ask them to try to be open to building a relationship with the horses and with us, the treatment team, based on trust, respect, and willingness. I drop in information about why we do what we do organically, as it presents itself, specific to each client's treatment needs. I'm inviting you to the same kind of experience. I feel that many of your questions will be answered naturally, through the stories I share in the pages ahead. However, for those who do like to have a working point of reference, photographer AJ Morey has assisted in writing an introduction that shares an outline of the conceptual framework that is Equine-Partnered Psychotherapy and Coaching. Note that we do not endeavor to provide a full description of all processes and how they work; nor do we list the numerous studies that now support this work. That remains for a subsequent book.

I invite you to proceed in the way that best works for you. If you are a reader who wants to get right to the stories, then skip forward to chapter 1 (p. 15) and save the introductory explanation for later. If you prefer to first have a basic understanding of the kind of Equine-

Partnered Psychotherapy and Coaching we use at Unbridled Change, then proceed with the Introduction. My overall challenge to you is the same challenge I give my clients: Put aside any preconceived notions about what you believe a horse is and what you think therapy is. Read the pages ahead with a "beginner's mind," open to the possibilities of "what if" in a good way.

The Power of Horses

Therapy empowers us to heal ourselves and make sense of the past. Sometimes that healing only happens on one plane—the mind. The stories in this book, however, present another way to heal the *whole person*—mind, body, and spirit all together. The "Horse Cure," to us, is defined as a means of correcting or relieving anything that is troublesome or detrimental. When you blend building an "in the moment" partnership with a real being, in this case a horse, with the different "mental health therapy" approaches and theories, the result is a powerful catalyst for change that integrates all the pieces of the self. Over the past 17-plus years I have watched client after client find a level of connection to the *authentic self*. Clients learn that their authentic selves are not some fantasy or dream of "who they could be," but rather a very real sense of self based on who they truly are *at their core*, free from the labels of the world and what they were told they *should* be. The power of partnering with horses helps us "cure ourselves" of our past and provides the opportunity to see, feel, and change—in the moment—any old, limiting beliefs that may be blocking us from who we truly are and who we want to be. Horses provide us the gift of awareness and an opportunity to try giving and receiving unconditional love. Through learning how to build a partnership-based relationship with horses, we are able to learn how to be okay with expressing our needs, holding boundaries, and learning a dance of communication based in love and connection versus power and control.

Working every day with horses as my co-therapists has been an honor. My hope for this book is that by the end you will see what I see every day: partnering with horses has the power to unlock our own innate healing ability so that *we can restore and cure ourselves.* This power isn't through magic or voodoo, but through the nature of horses and their desire to be at peace with the world around them.

This book takes you inside the healing journeys of some of our clients, as well as my own. Throughout I have changed the names and identifying situations/features of clients for their privacy. However, the changes that occurred during their sessions shared in the stories here are factual. It should be noted that the stories are told from my point of view, as the equine professional. I do not presume to speak for the clients or the horses. Instead, I share the impressions and thoughts I had of the interactions through the lens of my role in the sessions. (I do often use the plural pronouns "we" and "us" in the stories, when I am speaking of the Unbridled Change team or organization, which includes me, and photographer AJ Morey.) While I did my best to remember the dialogue accurately and have based the stories on notes and memories of the human team, I'm sure that some of it is filtered through my bias and understanding. I ask that you have an open heart to follow the intention of the stories. I'm not giving out advice or guidance on how to "do" equine-partnered therapy, nor is the intention for anyone to follow this book as medical or therapeutic advice. Please seek professional help if any part of this book triggers you and you need assistance.

Much of the work I do with Unbridled Change clients has no language and is instead embodied, relying on a physical connection between the horse and the client. I intend for the photographs, taken by AJ Morey, to inspire understanding that words alone may not achieve. (We have Temple Grandin to thank for originally explaining how people can see and understand much more like animals—in pictures.) Many of the horses in the photos are from Unbridled Change, but in order to honor the privacy of the clients, these are not pictures from the actual sessions described in the stories. Please also know that the horses in the photos are *real* horses, just as they are—they aren't airbrushed or polished for presentation. My hope is that the images capture moments and convey feelings to match the stories.

Chapters 1 through 3 trace the progress of three individuals and their therapeutic interactions with horses. Chapter 1 is a part of my personal journey, describing how a horse helped me reclaim my life after a devastating illness, and giving context for how and why I understand Unbridled Change clients and horses so keenly. Chapters 2 and 3 introduce you to two different individual clients—a child and an adult, respectively. They give you an intimate look into how horses respond to human distress and how humans grow from this interaction.

Chapters 4 through 7 are composed of snapshots of different individual client-focused stories explaining how relationships they had with horses have supported them in restoring pieces of their selves. Chapter 8 reflects upon why horses matter as relational beings, and what the stories in this book offer to our understanding of human-animal relationships. I review the insights about healing that are revealed in these pages and anticipate the next steps in the field of equine-assisted activities and therapies. And I share one last client story to close.

Now I invite you to explore why the horse cure can be a lasting, spiritually healing experience.

Michelle Holling-Brooks

Editor's Note: In the pages ahead, when referring to horses in a general sense, we have used masculine pronouns, not because we favor male horses over female, but to ensure clarity.

INTRODUCTION

The Horse Power of Stories: Equine-Partnered Psychotherapy and Coaching

By AJ Morey

*T*he Horse Cure is about how we can address and alleviate difficult emotional and mental conditions through the practice of Equine-Partnered Psychotherapy and Coaching (EPPC). "Cure" may seem like an audacious word to use, but we are invoking an abundant well of meanings in choosing this term to describe what Michelle Holling-Brooks is practicing at Unbridled Change. "Cure" originates from Latin, *cura* meaning the "spiritual charge of souls" or "spiritual care." From there its meaning flows through old French and Middle English, accruing further power as "care, healing, concern, and responsibility." Later "cure" comes to mean medical care or a remedy. In *The Horse Cure* we welcome the full range of meanings for the word. Equine-Partnered Psychotherapy and Coaching (EPPC) is a powerful approach to correct or relieve mental health issues and behavioral patterns that are detrimental and limiting. Or, to invoke the title, EPPC is a promising cure—an expression of spiritual care and healing—that partners horses with an equine specialist and a mental health specialist to create the space for human healing and growth. EPPC offers informed approaches and effective strategies for overcoming debilitating mental and physiological responses to what can sometimes feel like unbearable trauma.

The Horse Cure provides anecdotal evidence about this form of therapy to encourage conversation, advocacy, and further study. If you already have some background in equine-partnered therapies, or if you would prefer an unmediated experience with Michelle's stories about EPPC, you may choose to skip this chapter and begin with chapter 1 (p. 15). We are aware that readers will approach the book from many different places.

Michelle's invitation in the preface to read through the stories with a "beginner's mind" is a concept encapsulated by the Zen Buddhist term *Shoshin* (初心). Shoshin refers to embodying an attitude of openness and a lack of preconceptions when studying a topic, even when studying at an advanced level, just as a beginner would. The accounts she shares detail how clients generate their own stories about their life experiences through the partnership of the horses they meet in the arena. Those stories, and the process of making sense of them, become a bridge to building a new life.

From Horsemanship to Equine Therapies

Narratives about client-horse relationships and their goodness partakes of a respected tradition of ethology in animal studies that challenges the rigidity of the scientific model. Our world can only be enriched and improved by understanding that animals are sentient creatures with thoughts and emotions. As animals move from the traditional roles of "beasts of burden" and into various roles of companionship, it is possible that we are getting far more from animals than we are giving, but we look to create a world where more mutuality is the norm.

The story is the essential vehicle for pondering relationships. All the anecdotes deriving from the participant observers in the field testify to the intimacy between the animal and the human that arises when one creature encounters, watches, and responds to the other. The encounter, observation, and response goes in both directions; it is impossible not to feel the animal magnetism of the lives we are trying to understand, and for better and worse, they feel us in the same way. What we now understand is that animals gather their own insights about us and respond (photo 1). Their sensitivity to our thoughts and feelings is an indispensable part of the tale that unfolds between horses and humans. Just like other animals, horses respond intelligently and communicatively to human beings, and like us, they seek connection and meaningful relationships (photo 2).

Historically, the fantastic forms given the horse (Trojan horse, Pegasus) and the art celebrating the beauty of horses remind us that the horse is "a symbol of human aspiration and imagination" (Robles, 31), and there are countless books and films about horses, not to mention annual calendars. The horse industry—in all its forms, from racing to showing, pleasure riding to ranch work—is prolific with materials about how to train, ride, and otherwise enjoy or use the horse. The Mustangs of the American West have long been a cherished symbol of freedom (photo 3). Unfortunately, cultural fascination with horses hasn't always led to humane treatment, much less authentic relationships. Many horses still get treated as if they were insensate machines. How we treat animals in captivity, and otherwise, matters as much for our own humanity as for their lives.

Training of horses has taken on many different forms throughout the years, as well. There is currently a movement, which is gaining momentum, based on gaining a horse's cooperation rather than using coercion or domination. Many of these methods are derived from direct observations about how horses behave with each other when left in a herd environment. Today's horsemanship teaches humans to communicate with horses by learning to see as horses see, and to use our own body language in ways that will communicate effectively with the horse—both in giving and receiving signals. This communication works because humans are acknowledging the ways in which horses "speak" through body language and attempting to respond in kind (photo 4). It also works because horses are exquisitely attuned to their physical and emotional environments.

Michelle Holling-Brooks agrees with the philosophy of renowned trainer Carolyn Resnick that horses are open to following our leadership *when it is fair and just*. We are advised by many animal behavior experts that horses are prey animals and that their preternatural reflexes are part of the safety responses we have to overcome in order to ride them safely. While this statement is true, Michelle views it as only part of the picture. To her, the holistic picture is that *horses look for a leader*. Their choosing to accept us as their leaders is a key component in truly partnering with horses and thus being safe with them. They want to grow a bond with us, not only because they are herd and prey animals, but because they enjoy companionship and relationships. When we lead through gentleness, consistency, and with trust and respect, we can grow a strong working bond based on willingness and a desire for connection. This relationship is modeled on how horses form relationships in the wild, where they remain in family units and rely on those units to preserve safety and meet their needs. They might appease us by doing our bidding out of duty, but what we should aspire to is the magnetism of a trusting partnership that doesn't deny leadership but also doesn't depend upon a hierarchy of domination and control.

There are two important outcomes from this relationship-based approach to equine therapy. First is the recognition of the horse as an equal partner, healer, companion, or teacher. The horse in Equine-Partnered Psychotherapy and Coaching is not a tool or an instrument. EPPC practitioners don't "use" horses, they rely upon the horse's honest response to clients because they value the insights the horse can provide (photo 5). Second, treating horses with respect also means treating clients with respect. Clients are in charge of their own healing, and Michelle believes they have the insight to figure out what they need to reach their goals and find their own cure. In order to support the clients in their own healing, the horses, too, need to be empowered to make their own decisions about participation in this form of therapy—as partners, not as beasts of burden.

In short, EPPC developed because people with mental health therapy expertise *and* a respect for horses and what they can teach us about ourselves partnered together with empowered horses to create a space for human clients to find hope, healing, and personal growth. This birthed a way of "employing" horses as mental health facilitators in a fascinating new arena, variously called equine-assisted/facilitated/ guided learning, psychotherapy, counseling, trauma therapy, or education. Because there is no industry standard for the "employment" of equines in delivering mental health services and/or life coaching and wellness services, this book uses the designator that reflects Michelle Holling-Brooks' perspective, practice, and trademarked term: Equine-Partnered Psychotherapy and Coaching.

EPPC and Trauma

EPPC is an intense form of encounter between horse and human that is rooted in contemporary understandings of trauma, the neuroscience of mindfulness, and the executive functioning skills for modern life coaching and energy work. EPPC is premised on the understanding that horses have consciousness, cognition, and emotion, and that horses provide an essential partnership with humans in addressing trauma. Not every person who enters therapy or seeks support has suffered trauma. Clients also use counseling as a safe space for exploring ideas, effecting transitions, and coping with challenges, as EPPC can be effective for people struggling with "typical" life concerns. However, EPPC is known to address intractable and destructive wounds, events and experiences that require more insight than can be provided through guided self-reflection. These wounds populate a category of psychological distress that psychiatrists and clinicians still struggle to address meaningfully, despite our relatively sophisticated understanding of how such traumatic experiences can permanently reshape a personality. We now know enough about the biology of trauma to understand why neither talk therapy nor drug therapy, *nor both together*, are adequate solutions. Moreover, we know that the psychological and physical harm suffered by children in abusive situations has lasting effects on cognition and emotional stability.

In fact, there is no single therapy that can address the tentacles of post-traumatic stress (PTS) outcomes from trauma. Clinician Peter Levine is clear about the starting point. Therapists need to begin with "body-speak," not words, and then gradually access the emotional pathways that might lead to words and stories (45). The physical, visceral, bodily experience of trauma is "the body's narration" (49) that the therapist must recognize and address. In fact, articulate clients may use their verbal skills to block insight, substituting the comfort of verbiage for the discomfort of feeling deeply. In the case of trauma, "memories are fundamentally different from the stories we tell about the past. They are dissociated: the different sensations that entered the brain at the time of the trauma are not properly assembled into a story, a piece of autobiography" (van der Volk, 196). Equine-Partnered Psychotherapy, like many emerging animal therapies, is a critical tool in empowering clients to take charge of their health, encouraging them to reassemble the fragmented pieces of their experience into stories that bring coherence and purpose back into their world.

Horses may seem unlikely for this work. For some people, horses—with their long faces, big heavy feet, and powerful frames—don't seem all that approachable or intelligible. Perhaps because they don't have eyebrows or features that express emotions in the way we can read with dogs, horses have been mistaken as simply "dumb" (photo 6). Additionally, horses are large, strong, and foreign to most people. For nearly all clients this is challenging. Yet equine size and communication patterns, along with their emotional intelligence, make them remarkable partners in the mental health enterprise. The development of equine therapies has foregrounded something that sometimes doesn't seem obvious to outsiders: horses are intelligent, sentient animals. The client has to trust the treatment team, and that means trusting the horses, too. For the typical client, trust is a rare experience, and an essential foundation for healing.

Working with horses can repair a wounded mind, body, and spirit. It's an emotional or spiritual process coupled with physical activity. The physical activity component is crucial. Freeing the mind involves freeing the body. In the words of prominent psychotherapist Bessel A. van der Volk, "our research did not support the idea that language can substitute for action...As we will see, finding words to describe what has happened to you can be transformative, but it does not always abolish flashbacks or improve concentration, stimulate vital involvement in your life or reduce hypersensitivity to disappointments and perceived injuries" (196). EPPC is a therapy that embraces mute, physical experience and communication with a powerful, aware animal as an essential companion for insight, cognitive reflection, and emotional peace. It's a powerful strategy for helping clients find life-affirming tools for overcoming the effects of trauma.

What Happens in an EPPC Session?

As you will gather from the stories in this book, EPPC typically does not involve riding and should be distinguished from other horse-related therapies that *do* involve riding, such as therapeutic riding. EPPC practitioners may instruct clients in some aspects of horsemanship, but riding changes the dimensions of the therapy. Riding involves rules and specific skills, both of which are useful things to know, but which also inhibit the spontaneity and unmediated environment that can be created during an EPPC session. Riding has intrinsic value, just like the groundwork of EPPC; however, the timing and choice of when to bring it into a client's treatment plan requires a deft touch and must be a collaborative decision between the client, treatment team, and the horse partner. In Michelle's practice the shift to riding is an expansion of the client's goals into re-patterning of executive functioning skills and self-esteem.

The power of the EPPC session is that the client *and* the horse lead the session. A typical Equine-Partnered Psychotherapy session is facilitated by a mental health professional in collaboration with an equine professional, and both in partnership with a horse or horses. Simply put, EPPC involves putting a client into contact with a horse or horses on the ground, asking the client to build a relationship with the horse based on trust, respect, and willingness, and then processing the experience with the client. There is no riding involved in these first stages of EPPC. The goal for the client is not about horsemanship or coaching the client to a successful conclusion of whichever task might be the focus that session. Instead, the goal is to create a space for the client to see, feel, and experience how one inhabits relationships and where past, limiting beliefs and thought patterns are impacting the client currently. The goal is for someone who may be stuck, mental-health-wise, to learn to initiate problem-solving skills and manage various tasks on one's own. In that sense the only correct way to build a relationship with the horse is the one in which the horse *also* has a choice. Between observing and figuring out how to partner with a horse to complete a task, such as asking the horse to walk to a cone in the middle of the ring and back to the treatment team, 50 minutes may pass quickly. When the client returns to the team, an invitation to talk about the experience may be offered, but if the client doesn't want to, that's fine. EPPC does not require clients to articulate what may be happening. Some of the benefits of EPPC are that the client is (usually) outdoors, physically engaged, and *experiencing*—not necessarily talking. EPPC provides multiple opportunities to restore harmony between body and emotions, because physical movement, along with the sounds and sights and smells and touch of the horse, is so much part of the therapy.

During a session, while the mental health professional is observing the client, the equine professional is watching how the horse responds to the client. Horse body language is eloquent, and even in a "quieter" session, where nobody seems to do much of anything, minute gestures from the horse may tell an entire story. A horse walking to the corner and cocking his leg is something. A horse following the client around the arena is something. A horse walking away every time the client approaches, and then breathing out heavily when the client stands still, is something. What is said during a session can be important, but this is a therapy that does not depend upon a client being able to articulate every thought and emotion for its value. Clients too wrapped up in language, in fact, may be using words as a way to hide from the real story. During the processing of what is happening out in the arena with the horse, the treatment team may call the client's attention to how the horse has acted, doing so in the most neutral language possible, so that the team is not suggesting an interpretation to the client. "What do you think the horse was saying? Can you share what just happened with those two horses?" This approach makes every effort to allow the client's story and language to stay true to the client's perceptions and thought processes.

While having the client in essence "rewrite" a meaningful and empowering story or stories is the end goal of treatment, the result does not have to be a novel. All that needs to happen is that clients can see the pieces of their lives, from a detached observer role, in a narrative flow that makes sense and opens a path to new behavior and feelings. That can only happen if the clients are the ones who create the stories, in their own words, in their own time. Clients are able to do this because of the partnership they build with the horses (photo 7). Van der Volk—known for his research in the area of post-traumatic stress—says that "some people don't remember anyone they felt safe with. For them, engaging with horses may be much safer than dealing with human beings. [One client said that] having been entrusted with the responsibility for caring for a horse was the critical first step for her. Her growing bond with her horse helped her feel safe enough to begin to relate to the staff of the center and then to focus on her classes, take her SATs and be accepted to college" (215).

Horses respond to our emotions: anger, fear, heartbreak, defiance, pain, joy, excitement, and denial, just to name a few. How they respond to the array of emotions is as varied as emotions themselves. However, their response will often break through defensive barriers simply through physical presence. The horse's response guides the treatment team as well as the client by pointing the client to areas of psychological distress not immediately apparent or known. Horses do not "mirror" human emotions. If they did, sessions with troubled clients would be fruitless. Horses do *respond to* human emotions. Shannon Knapp— founder of Horse Sense of the Carolinas—describes the horse's role as "attunement" because what happens "more closely resembles a deep, instinctual listening of the horse to the emotional state and body language of the client, the same kind of deep presence horses seem to exhibit in every moment of their lives" (*More than a Mirror,* 294). What becomes miraculous for many clients is that this formidable animal is transformed through the encounter into a partner and trusted confidant. Clients often report how grateful they are that they can say and feel anything around a horse and not be judged. They learn how to communicate with horses as they learn how to communicate with themselves. If they can enter this arena with growing strength and trust, then they can re-enter the arena of their own lives with the same insight.

Steve

Here's an example of the power that comes from allowing clients to build their own stories with their own words. In a transcribed interview used with permission, Steve, a Vietnam veteran, described his first encounter with a small group of horses at an equine-assisted psychotherapy facility:

The horse experience was very stressful to begin with. I was very afraid. All I knew was that they'd stomp on you or bite you. To be thrown into the arena with all those horses my heart was beating 1,000 miles an hour. My survival mode was on, my flight was on, and I had to deal with it. Walking amongst them was in their territory, like in Vietnam. What did I have to do to survive this massive group of horses, not knowing anything about them? It took a lot for me to do that.

After Steve came home from the war, he didn't tell anyone what had happened while he was there. He spent years trying to heal himself by helping others through a street ministry. He blocked out the most agonizing parts of his own story, further isolating himself (a common coping mechanism of post-traumatic stress). What had happened in his body—fear, grief, physical injury—took up residence in his mind. In post-traumatic stress, what the mind understands about the lethal danger of a violent situation inhabits the responses of the physical self. It is a nightmarish imprisonment of the self by the body, rooted in our profoundly biological survival instincts. As demonstrated in the interview excerpt, Steve came to equine-assisted therapy with fear. Being with horses, to him, was almost like being asked to walk amidst the enemy.

One exercise Steve was assigned involved observing a group of horses, picking one to halter, and bringing the horse back to the therapeutic team. (Note that at Unbridled Change, a client would not be asked to halter a horse on a first visit, and maybe not even a third or fourth. Michelle would ensure that the client first developed a trust relationship with the horse without use of any restraints.) Steve picked a young mare named Gypsy. She exhibited a challenging attitude, like so many of the teenagers he had ministered to in the streets, so he felt they could become friends. Week after week, he walked with Gypsy, and he talked to her (photo 8). Steve could see that Gypsy did not act as if she would try to cause him harm, yet he still could not bring himself to put a halter on her.

Why was the halter such an issue for him? In Vietnam, Steve was a "tunnel rat." His job was to go into the intricate underground passages created by the enemy, find the Viet Cong, and then destroy the tunnels. Here he describes the lonely terror of darkness and confinement:

> *They had all kinds of booby traps when you went down, and you had to learn through experience. Feel was the big thing. And smell...that was important too.... In the beginning I'd only go about 10 feet, and then you started feeling and knowing, and your hearing became so intense and your smell.*

Steve's retelling shows a level of physical and mental paranoia that is appropriate for the situation; a mental state that is protective in context and destructive out of context. But his mind and body couldn't distinguish the present from the encoded memories of sound, smell, and touch, emanating from an imprisoning tunnel. It was a powerful memory disassociated from its original creation. Steve's traumatized imagination translated his "tunnel rat" experience into other situations—riding in a subway, being in a crowd, and putting the halter on Gypsy.

> *I couldn't put the halter on her. I couldn't do it because of those tunnels. You couldn't get out if you wanted to.... Things I didn't remember about Vietnam I'm just now remembering. I didn't want her to feel like she couldn't escape. I couldn't get out of the tunnels. I didn't want her to feel that, that she was being held like that. So I threw the rope over her neck and led her that way.*

When Steve was able to name *why* he was at an impasse with the haltering activity, he talked about being a "tunnel rat," which he had never discussed in any of his years meeting with Veterans Affairs doctors. Being able to acknowledge his tunnel experience in words was a significant step in his healing. The words appeared—not at once, but over time—because of a mute, physical experience with the horse, Gypsy. Once he had unlocked those words, he was thrilled to find that one day shortly thereafter, Gypsy rested her head on his shoulder and dozed.

This is Steve's story about what happened. His interpretation is completely valid. It's his experience. It's touching that his empathy with Gypsy was so acute as to render him unable to act when it came to the halter. He was with her and she with him. This connection allowed him to access another creative solution, affirming the emotions and thoughts he felt about himself in that moment.

Mutual Dignity

The mutual dignity of the horse and client is the essence of EPPC. Here is how Michelle Holling-Brooks describes her practice:

Over the past 15-plus years I have developed and fine-tuned EPPC sessions so that the horse, free from tack and constraints, is not just a prop but has a true voice to interact with the client. This approach sets the environment for the client to build the relationship and bond with the horse out of gentle leadership skills, rather than blunt approaches of power and control. In our approach the horse has the ability to say "yes," ignore the client, or say "no" by leaving the client. The client also has the same rights as the horse. The result is clients have the opportunity to become aware of what their body language is saying and what their personal needs and wants are inside the dance of relationship with the horses. The clients also have the space to reflect back. If they get a "maybe" or "no" from a horse, how will they respond? What limiting or negative beliefs are stopping them from personal growth? Clients learn the skills to make a "you-turn," like counselor, speaker, and author Mary O'Malley teaches in her book What's in the Way Is the Way.

A "you-turn" asks clients to look inward first, with curiosity and openness, to explore the "blocks" inside themselves first. Often the same things that are blocking them in the real world and keeping them from moving forward and being successful are the same things blocking them in the arena with a horse. The horse can be an amazing teacher for showing us what is hard to see in ourselves—the good...and the not-so-pretty parts. Clients can practice holding positive boundaries. Clients can practice being open with their heart and energy because the horse is not judging how they look, what clothes they wear, or what their past might have been.

In this book, Michelle Holling-Brooks tells one story after another, none of which can be replicated, but all with outcomes that can be verified by both client's and therapist's reports. Her accounts make every effort to give clients their full autonomy in creating their stories while honoring the uncanny roles of the horses. The accumulation of stories means something for our understanding about how EPPC works: we can become more critical and reflective about our practice, and advance our understanding of horse-facilitated healing.

In our own journeys as facilitators in the EPPC process, we have learned from horse trainers, as well as horse enthusiasts who promote the healing properties of horses and invite spiritual contemplation. We have learned from emerging literature about the efficacy of equine therapies, most presented in traditional, quantifiable language or through professional organizations. (We have provided appendices and a bibliography of the books most immediately informing *The Horse Cure* at the conclusion of this book.) All these resources have helped us grow, but perhaps most of all, we have learned from the horses and the stories they and clients have created through Equine-Partnered Psychotherapy and Coaching. We hope you'll find the same reward in these pages.

ONE

Schedule A: The Horse That Started the Journey

Michelle

When I was five years old, I went with my family on a guided trail ride through the canyons of Texas. I loved it and didn't want to get off the horse at the end of the ride. (My sister decided horses were not her thing at all.) After that, I continuously bugged my parents for riding lessons. My mom didn't need much convincing. She was an army BRAT (Born, Raised, And Transferred) and most of the army bases had stables. Horses had been a cherished part of her young life, and as an adult Mom valued the structure and confidence that riding had given her.

When I was diagnosed with dyslexia and attention deficit disorder with hyperactivity (ADHD), one of my doctors told my parents that horseback riding was a great way for me to learn self-regulation and focus. My mom discovered Full Cry Farm Junior Equitation School run by the renowned Jane Marshall Dillon, who wrote several books on equitation. I was turning seven, and Mrs. Dillon had a rule that she didn't take riders younger than eight years old, but she agreed to see me for a riding interview. I must have done something well because she accepted me into her program a year early. The move to her school set the foundation for my whole life.

I became the typical "barn rat," the affectionate term used to describe youngsters who just won't leave the barn and are willing to do pretty much anything to stay longer—mucking out stalls, sweeping cobwebs, cleaning tack, or brushing horses. My mother said I would beg to get to the stable early so I could make sure the horse was perfectly groomed, my tack was clean, and I was ready for roll call and inspection for proper riding habit from Mrs. Dillon. After the lessons I would stay for hours to do it all again.

I worked hard, and I was quickly moved up the ranks of "lesson horses" to Mrs. Dillon's personal mounts: Keynote and Schedule A. Only one or two riders a year were chosen to work with them. Keynote was Mrs. Dillon's riding horse and Schedule A belonged to her son. The summer I turned 13, I was completely devoted to riding Schedule (photo 9). I had no inkling how much things were about to change.

A Shocking Diagnosis

One day at the beginning of eighth grade, I asked to stay home from school because my head hurt and I felt sick to my stomach. By that evening my temperature had spiked over 104 degrees, and I was throwing up nonstop and unable to stand because of pain and lack of movement in my legs. My parents took me to urgent care, but the doctors there were alarmed because I could not move my neck or head without crying out from the excruciating pain. They told my parents to get me to the emergency room at the local hospital immediately; we should not wait for an ambulance because they were being used in a parade that evening in my hometown.

It was Halloween night, so my fragmented memories are a little like a cheesy "B" horror movie. The nurses and doctors were dressed in costumes and nothing made sense to me. They rushed me from place to place. I had an ice bath, a spinal tap, an MRI, and pain that no one could help with. They treated the symptoms while waiting for the results.

The diagnosis was viral eastern equine encephalitis (EEEV), which I'd gotten from a mosquito, probably at the farm. The encephalitis became further complicated because I'd contracted viral spinal meningitis at the same time. The result of the two diseases together meant a severely compromised body and brain. The encephalitis caused my brain to swell outward while the spinal meningitis caused the fluid and lining of my brain stem and spinal cord to swell inward. As a result of this severe swelling, I slipped into a coma for seven days. During that time the doctors prepared my parents for all possible outcomes—I might be fine, or I might not wake up. I might be brain damaged and physically impaired, or I could die.

I don't remember any of this period, following my diagnosis. What I do remember clearly is waking.

I opened my eyes and everything was crazy bright and overwhelming. It was also very blurry. I saw a mass of "pink" in front of me. I say "pink" because at the time I no longer could access words for what I was seeing and feeling. My working memory for labeling things was gone. (The pink mass turned out to be what had been a favorite, oversized stuffed animal I had called "Flopsie" prior to my illness.) I could only hear faint muffled sounds; they had no meaning to me. I remember a mass of shadows started whipping around me, touching me. I didn't understand that it was people who were grabbing my body. My first post-illness memory is of a gripping sense of fear, overwhelm, and confusion that seemed to take up permanent residence in the coming years.

And the people I didn't recognize who were surrounding me? Sadly, they were my mother, my sister, and my father. I didn't know any of them because I didn't know myself. I didn't know I was a person, let alone who I was in relationship to a world I didn't understand. While I was comatose and battling for my life, the swelling on the outside and inside of my brain damaged my memory and optical centers, as well as my motor skills. The fluid and scar tissue also impacted my hearing. Everything sounded as if I was deep underwater. I had extreme light sensitivity, so I refused to open my eyes. The only thing I could handle was complete darkness. I could not move my body from about the middle of my back down, although I could sense a touch on my lower body, the kind of pressure you might feel if your lip is numb at the dentist.

I can still recall the physical sensations and feelings that accompanied the illness: pain, fear, dread, terror, and an overwhelming sense that I was alone. I felt like I wasn't doing the things that people really wanted me to do, and I thought something was deeply wrong with me.

Most of All, I Hurt

Now, when I look back I compare that time in my life to what I believe it must be like to be born, but with one huge difference: A newborn's memory and body rhythms actually start to develop while in utero. During the nine months of pregnancy the baby is able to "sync" to the mother's heart rate and her patterns of breath and movement. A fetus also begins to recognize voices, and neuropathways begin to form that predispose a connection to biological family. I didn't have the familiar voices and heart rhythms of my family to ground me. Those pathways had been erased. I didn't even have my own body rhythms and vital signs to connect with because they had become irregular and incoherent due to the swelling and damage to my parasympathetic nervous system. Everything overwhelmed me. I was stuck in a body that hurt so much I continually let out guttural screams.

Because I couldn't remember anything else, my brain decided this state was normal: I developed a belief system based solely on my understanding that life was pain, fear, and helplessness. The brain needs to compare and draw conclusions from past events to make sense of current situations. This constant comparison of the present to what you have learned in the past also gives you a sense of ease and comfort in the familiar. Without the connections of past memories to help guide me, my brain could only draw on what was happening in the moment. And because I had no sense of time, every moment felt like it had no end. My days were filled with confusion as people I didn't recognize kept coming into my space, crying, and touching me. I couldn't get away. I was trapped in the bed. So I learned to look away or close my eyes. When I opened them again, they were still there. I felt horrible. I somehow knew these people wanted something from me, but I didn't understand them.

However, I did begin to understand the people who followed the same routine around me—the nurses. They brought me food, performed a task, or sometimes used needles that hurt, but then they left. If I was uncomfortable or needed to be moved, I learned to push a button. Then one of the nurses would come, look at me, and figure it out. Most of all, I hurt. As much as possible, I kept my eyes closed and head turned away into Flopsie, my protector.

My mother, father, and sister didn't have a routine. What they wanted from me was so much harder to figure out than what the hospital staff wanted. Because no one typically survived the kind of illness I had, nobody knew how to help my family deal with the questions that naturally came during my recovery process: What happens when the data of a person's whole life has been erased? What happens to those who love a person who is, in a sense, "gone," but is also still physically visible and alive in front of them? What happens to their knowledge and expectations of the person that were based on their own memories from the past?

My family longed for me to recognize and embrace them. I felt the force of their yearning, but I couldn't understand it or know how to respond. As time went and my hearing started to come back, I watched their lips moving, emitting garbled sounds, but I didn't know what any of it meant. I became more and more frustrated with them each time they tried to show me a picture. I didn't know what it was, only that they desperately wanted me to focus on it. I often shoved them away, or if they placed a photo in my hands, I would throw it as far as I could. I had a new emotion joining my pain, confusion, and fear.

Welcome anger.

Fighting

Once anger came into my world I unleashed it on anyone and every-one. I fought against being touched. I fought against going to physical therapy. I even fought eating. But everyone else always won. I couldn't move my body but they could. I weighed nothing. I had grown 4 inches while in the hospital and my legs were skinny from not being used.

I eventually gave up fighting on the outside and went totally limp. Because I didn't have memory of body awareness, it was easy for me to check out. All I had to do was close my eyes. By "shutting off my body" I could stop receiving information from the outside world and stop feeling.

Then one day the nurses helped my family pack everything up in my hospital room, dress me, and put me in a wheelchair. I was wheeled outside for the first time in months. The light was painful, and my head throbbed from sitting upright for so long. My parents placed me in a car. I was scared because I didn't understand what was happening, so I fought and pushed with my hands. They were taking me away from the only safe place I knew—the hospital—and bringing me home. But I didn't know what "home" was.

I was taken into a room—"my room." But I didn't know this room. I felt alone in this room. There was no button to call for someone if I hurt or was hungry. There were no predictable people who could figure out what I needed and then leave. Ironically, I wanted to be left alone, but I was terrified of being alone. The room symbolized to me being cut off from everything. Worse, it haunted me, because it was full of things I didn't know but things others expected that I would, or should, recognize: ribbons on the wall, stuffed animals, and pictures of faces—even ones that looked like me. But I couldn't remember any of it.

After being home for about three months I still refused to do anything—physical therapy, occupational therapy, schoolwork. I resisted any relationships. I didn't want to see or try to communicate or reconnect with my family or friends. I was so angry. The word "remember" became a four-letter word to me; it was an instant trigger for me to enter fight mode for many years to come. The more my family tried to reach me, the more I became overwhelmed by the feeling that I was not right, that I was not good enough. I felt that everyone wanted me to be "Michelle," but I didn't know who that was. I hated that "Michelle" because she represented an ideal I couldn't recall or emulate. I came to feel that I didn't have a right to be alive. I had somehow stolen this other girl's life. I was an imposter and a fraud.

Schedule A

I didn't know that my parents were having an ongoing argument behind the scenes. My mother wanted to take me to the barn and the horses. She knew that horses were what I had been connected to the most outside of my family. She also knew that horses had been known to help people with various needs through therapeutic riding. My dad argued against the idea. After all, it was being around horses in the first place that exposed me to the viruses that had resulted in so much suffering for everyone. He didn't want to risk enduring anything like it again. He wanted to keep me safe.

Fortunately, my mom won the argument.

It was still cool, so it must have been early spring when they packed me up and took me on a car ride. I could now somewhat hear out of my right ear, although not very well. I could also tolerate some light but only with sunglasses. I still had no motor control from the middle of my back down. I looked out the window. I knew if I didn't make eye contact then no one could get my attention and ask anything of me. I had perfected an ability to pretend that no one existed on earth except me.

During my recovery at home I had seen pictures of horses, and there were plastic ones in my room. However, on this side of my coma, I had never seen one in real life. When we pulled up outside a barn, I perked up but was still holding onto my anger. My parents placed me in my wheelchair; I tried to pretend I wasn't that interested as they wheeled me around the corner of the stable. By this point Mrs. Dillon had sold Full Cry Farm in Vienna, Virginia, where I had started taking lessons, and had relocated to a smaller facility nearby, which she named "Little Full Cry." The main barn was still pretty big! About 20 stalls lined both sides of the aisle, and of course it was full of large, beautiful horses. They poked their faces out over their Dutch stall doors; it looked like a sea of horse heads to me. The light flittered through the windows, catching the specks of dust that were floating in the air. I could smell the hay and the animals, and there was a sense of *something familiar*.

This was the first time since my illness that something had felt this way—like I knew it. I scanned the barn and looked back and forth at the horses and the stalls.

One horse in particular immediately caught my attention. I cannot put the sensation that came over me into words. I can only say that I felt a deep "knowing" and a bodily draw toward him on a cellular level. I knew that somehow I was connected to this one horse.

It was Schedule A.

"Schedgy," I said out loud—his nickname.

Up to this point, I had refused to speak. My parents had even started to try and teach me sign language because my doctors had not been able to determine whether they were dealing with a physical issue or a behavioral one. But I was making a choice not to speak. It was another way I felt I could control some part of my world.

I wheeled myself over to Schedgy's stall door and stopped. I wasn't really sure what to do next. I was afraid to reach my hand out. As far as I knew, I had never extended my hand to touch another living thing in my life. I sat there gazing up at the bay horse, looking into his large brown eyes and seeing a reflection of myself in them. He lowered his head to me. Blew into my ear. Nuzzled my face with his velvet-soft nose. He then moved forward, hitting the stall door with his massive chest. Schedgy stretched his long neck out and extended it over my shoulder. Placing his jaw on my back, he gently pulled me closer, toward his stall. He was giving me a hug (photo 10). I don't know how long we stayed that way. To me, it seemed like a lifetime.

I didn't brace against the big horse or shove him away like I did with everyone else. I was open to his touch. I remembered him! I wanted nothing more than to stay right where I was, wrapped round by his neck with his massive head protecting me and holding me. *I was home.* I felt whole. I didn't feel like an imposter in someone else's life. In that moment I felt fine just the way I was. His heart rate changed mine. His biorhythms were strong enough to slow mine down, giving me a sense of ease that I had not experienced since the onset of my illness. The high-strung, 17-hand jumper seemed an unlikely source of peace, and yet this was exactly what I felt. It was not just a physiological effect; it was also a spiritual moment that came together with his embrace.

I don't know what my parents felt in that moment. Now, as a mom, I can only imagine the huge mix of emotions they surely experienced: relief that I finally showed interest in something, that I could speak, but hurt by the fact that I could remember a horse and not them. Fortunately, they somehow managed to put their own feelings aside and embraced the idea that Schedule A was the only way to reach me.

My mom talked to my instructors about how to get me on a horse. Certainly one immediate issue was figuring out how to keep me in the saddle when my lower body had no movement. If I became unbalanced there was no safety net. If I fell I would just keep going until I hit the ground. While I weighed next to nothing, I was close to 6 feet tall at the time—my body was a lot harder to manage than that of a six-year-old. This wasn't a therapeutic riding barn with trained staff and side-walkers, so the farm staff came up with what seemed like a good solution at the time: They tied me to the saddle.

Note that this is not something I recommend! Do not ever tie a person to a saddle! But having said this, I have to confess that their makeshift solution was exactly the right thing for me.

Progress

Schedule A took great care of me. The staff started by leading me around. My instructors, Mary Lou and Janet, were pretty sly about working communication and social skills into the mix when I was riding. I had to look at the instructor or she would stop my horse. So I agreed to acknowledge humans because they controlled my ability to get what I wanted most: Schedule A.

I rode three to four times a week. Slowly my trunk control started to improve, and my instructors started to let me go independently around the ring. Then they let me trot—I felt like I was flying!

Every time I was around the horses I felt free.

Schedgy also gave me something else: Within six months of riding again, I started being able to move my legs and work toward bearing weight on them. Six months after that, I was running and trying out for my freshman basketball team.

How did riding do that? The neuroscience field was just barely out of its infancy in the early 1990s, so my doctors could not explain why riding a horse was "healing" the damage in my brain. We know now that the repetitive rhythmic motion of the horse moving my trunk and legs was a similar movement to the human walking gait. It was this repetition and the related firing of neurons in my brain and brain stem that enabled them to heal, forming new pathways around the ones that were damaged to match the input my brain was receiving from my body. There is a saying now that "neurons that fire together, bond together." With the repetition of firing neurons, my brain was able to see that some pathways were not connected and went to work building new routes to reconnect the firing neurons with the signals my body was sending it—that of the walking motion.

Schedule A gave me back my legs, and he gave me a safe place to find the "new me." During the year following my first day back on a horse, I relearned everything: how to walk, tie my shoes, read, spell, and do math. Some of these skills came back easily, and others were a struggle. I never regained my memories, though. The one anchor I had in what was often a sea of chaos was my connection to horses.

Safe Haven

Looking back now, I realize that in addition to reestablishing pathways for physical movement, I was lighting up new emotional pathways, as well. At the barn I felt calm, happy, and safe. But at home, the feelings established in the hospital were still in full swing: I felt like I was constantly under attack. My family could see my bodily recovery, and they were eagerly hoping I'd begin to show the same recovery in my mind. I thought they still wanted to "fix" me, and I was constantly fighting to have my new voice heard. I never seemed to be able to outrun the ghost of the mysterious past "Michelle." I still felt like I was not good enough, so I invented a belief system to go with my dysregulated feelings: I believed that the "real" Michelle died the day I woke up. I had stolen the place of this family's beloved little girl. This family (*my family*) was left with a girl who didn't know them, a fake daughter—hiding behind a mask of someone they loved.

School was also difficult, despite my regaining cognitive ability (math, writing, reading, and so on). My friends tried really hard, but I was not willing to believe they liked me. I didn't like me, so why would they? My best defense was to become a chameleon of sorts. I became a master at blending in with whatever group I was with. Band, jocks, nerds, goths, and gangs—they all liked me because I switched to match each group. Yet I had no *core*…no core me and no core group of friends. I floated from group to group; any time I hit a roadblock in one group, off I went to another.

The barn continued to be my safe haven. It was the one place I didn't have to morph and put on a fake mask. I quickly gained back everything that I had lost when it came to horses and riding. Plus, I gained something new! I gained the ability to connect with the horses on a nonverbal level. I could feel the slightest shift of their weight under me. I began to know what the horse needed from me to help him move the way I wanted. I like to joke now that English wasn't my first language—it was "horse." Because I couldn't hear for the first couple years after my illness, I learned to watch and read people's bodies and "feel the energy" of them. My own constant state of fight or flight also improved my skills of honing in on and reading micro-expressions as cues on what I should be doing or feeling. The skill of being acutely aware of nonverbal communication in humans was of amazing benefit when it came to reading and gathering information from a horse. I think this translated to the horses so easily because to me, unlike humans, horses always "matched," meaning that a horse always acted as he was feeling, and I could see how his physical motion and feelings were congruent. If I didn't acknowledge the horse's movements, it didn't go over well. I would get stuck in the corner of the arena, or my horse would walk off and not respond to my rein aids. But if I said, "I see you, I hear you, what do you need?" the horse would let out a breath and then respond in kind with acceptance and understanding.

One of my favorite memories of sheer joy was during a cross-country lesson. We had been working on bank jumps followed by a gallop to a combination. A bank is an obstacle that you jump up onto, canter on top of (for typically a stride or so), and then jump down "off" again. It is often preceded or followed by a vertical jump to test if you and the horse are connected and working together. Any misstep or bad communication could lead to a disastrous landing for horse and rider.

Schedule A and I were totally in sync. I barely had to touch my reins, and he was responding to just a squeeze of my fingertips. Slight shifts of my weight and leg cues would turn him at high speeds. I trusted him not to drag me to the jumps, and he trusted me not to put him in a bad spot. My instructor at this time, Janet, embodied the well-rounded teacher. She had a wealth of knowledge and also knew how to make the process of learning fun. She turned to us after a few practice rounds and suggested we ride out into the field as a group and herd the geese out of the way. The next minutes on Schedgy's back were nothing short of miraculous to me. I think it was the first time I really let a horse open up fully from a place of sheer energy. He turned with just a thought and sped up with just a shift of my weight forward. The other students and I were calling to each other and making a plan of "attack," laughing and galloping abreast, full tilt through a huge open pasture. Our horses' ears were perked toward the geese (who flew off before we got to them), and we made a huge loop and headed back to Janet. We never took it out of high gear.

I had no idea what flying could feel like before that moment.

I was hooked! From that point forward, I wanted that same feeling of being free and yet also connected to another being every time I interacted with a horse. In that moment I felt in every fiber of my being what it was like to be linked to someone else without terror or a struggle for control. I didn't trust in human connections because I had not felt a sense of true partnership with another person…yet. The human brain, body, and soul are not designed to function and thrive without connection to others. Serving this purpose, horses became my lifeline, providing acceptance and partnership. If I didn't feel a connection with my horse, I would stop and see what was missing. I didn't want a horse to follow me because I pulled on him or caused him fear. I knew how that felt all too well. I lived most of my day-to-day world "obeying" the wills of others to prevent possible pain. I didn't want to do that to a horse. I hadn't yet developed enough sense of self to project this new form of connection to humans, but I could ensure that I didn't make a horse feel the way the rest of the world made me feel.

The day we chased the geese was also when I figured out that I saw and felt horses differently than most people. I wanted the relationship with Schedgy first; the great performance was a very happy outcome of that relationship. I was surprised when I talked with other riders about this idea, and they looked at me like I had five heads. They agreed the gallop in the field was fun, but for them it was because they went *fast*. Fast on horseback was cool, yes, but that wasn't what I'd fallen in love with that day. Janet was the only one who seemed to understand that it had been the feeling of complete oneness with my horse that made me feel like I was flying. She smiled at me when I tried to explain. She winked and told me that I had found what takes most horsemen a lifetime to find—horses want connection and a relationship first and foremost (photo 11).

I began riding other horses besides Schedule A, helping retrain Mrs. Dillon's new lesson horses, but even after he was retired, Schedgy was my go-to safe-space. If I had a bad day at school or was upset for any reason, I would find him in his field or stall and share my thoughts. Schedule A made sense to me. When I talked with him, I felt that he could see the *real me*, the person that I hid from everyone, behind masks, out of fear of rejection. Every day I still worried I was a fraud, a fake—I felt like almost a shadow of a person. But when I was with him, and other horses, I didn't feel that way. They grounded me. They didn't judge me. They didn't compare me to anyone else.

Horses challenged me to be real, to be trustworthy, to not act out of anger, to ask, to not demand things for no reason. If I could do those things and listen to them, they would, in turn, show me trust, respect, love, connection, and willingness by following my lead when asked. Neither of us expected perfection from the other, but we did expect the other to put our connection as partners first and any corrections second.

I have enjoyed the love of several good horses since Schedule A, but his great heart marks the spot where I was able to reclaim my first connection to the "real me" and my courage. Years of growth, standing still, losing ground, and growing again have brought me to the magic moment where I am now. Fear is still here, as is the inner voice that whispers that I am still a fake—that I'm not real enough to speak. So, as I write this book, I say, "Hello, Fear, my old friend. Come sit next to me. Thank you for trying to keep me safe. But my desire to share the lasting change and healing that can occur in partnership with horses is greater than your power over me.

"You can sit and watch, but you are not taking over today."

I have shared this part of my story because I see pieces of myself in my horses and clients at Unbridled Change. I bucked and reared and lashed out when people got too close. I shut down when I couldn't cope with what relationships demanded from me. Like them, I have been hurt, bewildered, angry, and terrified by life experiences. My horses, clients, and I have some common ground. We are here to say, authentically, that *there is hope*. It's not because I am extraordinary. I'm not. I believe healing and change can come to anyone; all it takes is learning the foundations of trust, self-respect, and willingness. I believe anyone can develop these skills and pathways given the right circumstances and the right horses.

TWO

Cocoa and Radar:
Learning to Trust
Ashley

Working with horses for me is all about building a partnership, not performance. Therapeutic and personal growth activities with horses, where the focus is on mental health and development of the human rather than horsemanship skills, are also based on the human and horse developing confidence in each other, as well as willing movements of their bodies and minds in concert. Both approaches boil down to learning the "dance of trust." This is the art of communicating both internally with yourself and outside with others based on saying what you mean and meaning what you say—showing that you are predictable and that you are going to "show up" in a concurrent manner. At Unbridled Change, we have a little statement that helps break down the dance of trust for our clients: *If I can predict you 93 percent of the time, then I can trust you. If you break my trust but you work to "repair" any breaks in that trust in a fair and just way, then I can respect you. Once I trust and respect you, then I'm willing to be open to building a relationship with you based on connection instead of compliance and submission.*

Schedule A and I created a trust-dance that helped me repair and create secure attachments. Daniel J. Siegel shares in his work *A Journey to the Heart of Being Human* how you can actively choose to change your "attachment style" (the model of attachment that influences how you react to your needs and how you go about getting them met), but first you need to have awareness of your habitual responses and accept yourself for having those responses. Only then can you make an active choice to move forward with a new habit. As you practice the new behavior pattern you can slowly change your default and move toward an earned secure attachment with love (most people's default style is *not* secure). For me, horses have been my greatest teachers for building secure attachments. I strive to offer my clients the same feeling of safety that horses have given me.

A Difficult History

One young girl we worked with at Unbridled Change struggled with the dance of trust. "Ashley" was referred to us from the Department of Social Services. She was 11 at the time she started working with us and coming out of a residential treatment center. While she was there her goals focused on anger management and reducing destructive behaviors. Prior to being placed in the program she had become extremely violent with her adoptive mom and biological younger sister (her biological mother was not in the picture at all). These behaviors included hitting, kicking, verbal abuse, and even threatening to kill them with sharp objects, like knives. While at the residential program, Ashley had done some really good work on impulse control but was still struggling with repairing the relationship with her adoptive family. The county decided the best solution was to place her into foster care rather than sending her straight home. This "step-down process" allowed her to be out of a residential setting and have access to longer visits with her adoptive mom and sister in preparation for their reunification.

The court referred Ashley's case to us. We worked individually with both Ashley and her adoptive mom, "Kari." Ashley needed to confront her own attachment issues and work on fine-tuning her ability to self-regulate. Kari had concerns about how to parent Ashley, some of which were specifically associated with post-traumatic memories of how violent and out-of-control Ashley had been prior to being removed by the county. Once Ashley and Kari arrived at a healthier space as individuals, we would put Kari and Ashley together in family therapy, so both could learn how to function as a family without getting caught up in the past. We were familiar with the whole process—it typically takes nine to twelve months.

Ashley's history would churn your stomach. She had been removed from her biological home along with her siblings when she was around three years old. Social workers had found her locked in a closet. From what they could decipher the family had systematically abused her physically and sexually and neglected her needs. She was basically feral when she was placed in a foster home. Her foster mother, Kari, adopted Ashley and her younger sister once parental rights were terminated.

Ashley was diagnosed with reactive attachment disorder, post-traumatic stress (PTS), and oppositional defiant disorder (ODD). She was legally blind without her glasses and had a degenerative eye disorder that, according to doctors, would eventually take her sight altogether, and she had mild cerebral palsy, which affected her gait and mobility. She had learning disabilities as well: she was diagnosed with autism on the high-functioning end of the spectrum, nonverbal learning disorder, and attention deficit hyperactivity disorder (ADHD). Doctors had placed her on a cocktail of drugs to help her cope with all these labels and manage her impulses. The unique combination of physical and emotional presenting issues led the county to search for alternatives to traditional talk therapy, and Ashley's play therapist recommended Equine-Partnered Psychotherapy because it would help teach the relationship and self-regulation skills in a concrete, experiential, therapeutic environment.

The Whirlwind

On our first meeting Ashley came into our office like a whirlwind. She was tall for an 11-year-old, and skinny, with her dirty blond hair haphazardly pulled up into a ponytail. Her clothes were disheveled as well. Her case manager from the local community services board, "Barbara," had brought her and was trying to encourage Ashley to sit down at our main table in our office space where we chatted with people before going out into the arena. Ashley was not about to sit still. Instead she ran into my office, coming straight in without knocking.

"Who are you? Is this your office? Are you going to show me the horses? I like horses!" Ashley's questions flew out of her mouth as she pushed her way in and looked around at the various pictures and items I had on the wall. Before I had a chance to respond or even introduce myself she whirled back out, and scampered around the corner. Barbara once again tried to redirect her to sit down and wait for Cami, our mental health therapist, and me to join them at the table. Ashley realized there was a second office space and pushed into Cami's room, issuing the same machine gun sequence of questions without a pause.

Amused, I thought to myself that impulse control and social cues might be a good place to start!

I walked out of my office and sat down at the table, saying, "Ashley, is it? Would you like to join us at the table? Before we can go out with the horses we need to talk. This is the boring stuff we need to get through before we can get to the fun stuff in the arena." I paused to see if she would respond to the request. Nope, instead she started for the office door. "Ashley, can you please join us at the table? You don't need to sit down, but I do need your attention so we can get through this office stuff first." There it was. In the first few moments of our interaction I had put out a request. Now we would see how Ashley did with direct requests.

For those of us who struggle with attachment issues, even a simple request can be a psychological land mine. When I was reconnecting with Schedule A, I didn't want to request anything of him, not because I didn't want to have a relationship, but, ironically, because I did. If I asked something from him and he refused, or responded badly, I could be hurt. With a horse, it is possible to be hurt physically, but to me the bigger threat was the potential emotional pain of having him refuse or ignore my request. So, like a lot of people with attachment issues, I learned to reject any and all requests, even if you were just asking me what I wanted for lunch. Later in life, after a lot of work, and growing awareness of my own attachment style cycle, I was able to override my default and instead go to a more "secure" style response. I learned to embrace requests as opportunities to grow my relationships, not as threats. The big question was whether Ashley had developed a similar awareness and skills at her young age. We might find out with my simple request, "Please join us at the table."

I left some wiggle room in the request on purpose—I did not care if she sat down at the table, just that she joined us and gave me her attention for a quick second. I designed the request this way to give her a sense of control while still agreeing to complete it. Ashley and I were about to take our first step in our dance of building a relationship: Could she trust me to stick with what I said? Or could she get me to back off? If I abandoned my request for her to participate in our intake session before seeing the horses, I would signal that I wasn't trustworthy. If I was unreliable, if my actions and subsequent words weren't consistent, and if I didn't stick with my request, I would be unpredictable, and therefore, untrustworthy. If I was untrustworthy, Ashley could walk away from our relationship feeling secure in her intuition that I wasn't safe.

Cami and Barbara took a back seat in the room and left it up to Ashley and me to figure it out. Ashley judged me untrustworthy and made for the door.

Now, our office door is sticky, and given her sporadic movements, I knew it was going to be a challenge for Ashley to open. She pushed and pulled in short bursts, not slowing down long enough to give the door a chance to unstick.

"Wow! You guys lock your doors around here. Barbara, did you tell them I'm a runner? This is just like the place I came from. They locked their doors too, that way we couldn't run. I want to see the horses. You can talk to me then." Ashley moved to the bench behind the table and kneeled, looking through the large observational windows we have that face onto the arena.

A great deal of therapy is about going with the flow and direction of the client, and her movement was close enough to the table for me. "Thanks for joining us. My name is Michelle, and I have a couple of roles here. One, I'm the director and started this place. My second job here is that I'm the 'horsey person'—I'm in charge of the horses and what things we do with them during your therapy sessions." I paused.

Ashley turned, looked at me, and smiled. "Hi! So you are the person that can go get me a horse?"

"Yes, I am. However, first we need to finish our intake session." Shrugging my shoulders and bringing a look of disappointment to my face I added, "Sorry, but insurance requires me to go through all this before I can take you out to see the horses. I'm sure from being at the residential program you know the drill. The sooner we can get through this part the sooner we get out to see some horses. Deal?" In this statement, I conveyed a direct request, along with an expectation and a prompt for her to say "yes" or "no." This might not sound like a declaration of war to most people, but to Ashley, it might have well been. To her, this size of a request meant danger. If she decided to comply and listen, it meant she was willing to give us control, and in the past, giving anyone control was bad news for her.

So we waited.

Ashley lost her smile and looked around the office space. She looked back at the glass windows behind her. She looked at the solid door that led to the outside of the building. She then glanced at the set of stairs. Still kneeling on the bench she pointed at the staircase. "Where does that go?"

"Up to the second floor where we have a larger classroom area for big groups." Again I waited. I was trying not to add any more pressure to my original request to participate with the short intake.

She looked at the walls and saw drawings pinned to a bulletin board. "What are those?"

"Pictures that other clients have drawn for us."

"Can I draw you guys a picture while you talk?"

"Sure, I happen to have some crayons and an activity book right here."

With that Ashley turned around and sat down next to Barbara, her shoulder touching her case worker's arm, picked up a crayon and started coloring.

I resumed. "Okay, where was I? Oh yeah. This person sitting next to me is Cami. She is our 'people person' or therapist. She and I work together as a team along with our horses during your sessions." I went on to explain our program, especially how we wouldn't be like "regular" office therapy. "So the big difference is that we don't spend too much time here in the office talking. You do start in here every week. Since it will have been a week since we talked with you, we'll do a quick check-in: How was your week? Did anything happen that you want to share with us? All the good stuff, as well as if you had any what we call 'bumps in the road.' Once we are all caught up, out we go to spend time with the horses. That brings me to the next thing: In our program we ask you to build a friendship with different horses. So when you are working with the horses, we are working on your friendship—how the horse feels around you and how you feel about the horse. As the friendship grows, you and the horse will be able to do more and more together."

"So, like, if they trust me or not?" Ashley didn't stop coloring or even look up.

I thought to myself how thankful I was for all the therapy work she had done at the residential program. We didn't have to start from scratch.

"Yes, you got it. We aren't going to be teaching you horsemanship because it isn't about the 'right' way to work with a horse." I raised my hands in the air and made little quote marks around "right." Ashley lifted her head to follow the movement of my arms and for a brief second made eye contact with me. I continued. "So there really is no right or wrong way of doing things out here as long as you are not hurting yourself, hurting one of the horses, or hurting one of us. Does that work?"

Ashley shifted her weight. Looking from me to Cami and then finally at her case worker. "I guess. Are we done now?"

"I think so. Just to double check: If I say, 'FREEZE!' because I think someone is about to make an unsafe choice, what do I need you to do?"

"Stop and freeze. Got it. Horses!" Once again a huge smile spread over Ashley's face. She was practically bouncing out of her seat. I didn't think we were going to get much more out of our intake, and I was very pleased that she had given me the level of respect she did. "Okay, *now*, we can go meet some horses. Please stay with me so I can tell you all about them."

Ashley leaped from the bench with excitement. She knocked into the table and sent the box of crayons flying across the table and they scattered. Immediately she froze. She backed into Barbara with a look of terror on her face, wailing, "I didn't do that!"

"No worries." I smiled. "The crayons will be here when we get back. Let's go meet some horses." With that I opened the door and walked out of the office, motioning for her to join me as I walked to the arena.

Ashley looked at Barbara, who said, "Go on. We can clean this up after you meet them." Ashley looked at the table again, then at Cami and Barbara standing in the doorway. You could tell she was trying to process our reactions. From the little bit about her past we knew, I can only imagine how people with authority over her had reacted when she made a mistake. From the look of terror and now confusion on her face, we hadn't responded the way she thought we would. Apparently, we had broken a pattern. In that moment she had to come up with a new pattern or way of interacting with us that sidelined her usual default way of thinking. Because we broke her old pattern of expectations, she didn't have a pre-existing pathway in her thinking for interacting with people who were not mad, blaming, or punitive if she made a mistake. Our reaction was causing her to develop a new pathway for learning how to trust.

I know what comes after a new pathway—pushback from the old pattern. So I wanted our experience to continue before Ashley had an impulse to take back her willingness to connect with us. The best way to do that was to meet the horses.

After seeing her high energy but lower impulse control, I figured the pony herd would be the best fit for her. They tended to handle that combination better than our "big boy" horses who were quicker to defend themselves if they felt threatened. Out of the pony herd (Captain Hook, Red, Cookie, Squire, Cocoa Puff, and Sola) Cocoa Puff was the one that was drawn to Ashley. We weren't surprised (photo 12).

Cocoa Puff

Cocoa came to us as a fostering situation. She had been "adopted" by a family from a sale of Mount Rogers wild ponies (two herds roam the Mount Rogers National Recreation Area in Virginia). But the family didn't have prior horse experience and didn't know what to do with a wild, three-year-old pony. Because she was small, they tried to handle her wildness by harshly controlling her environment and physically overpowering her. The result was when she came to our barn, she was severely untrusting. She was so reactive to movements that the only place she would stop shaking was in a stall—her one place of refuge. When we tried to turn her out in a paddock she would run without stopping until she finally ended up lathered in a sweat, backed into a corner. For three months I sat with Cocoa in a large box stall. Only after she finally saw and accepted I wasn't a threat did she come to me freely. But once I moved her into the mare and foal paddock we had to repeat the same process all over again. It took around eight months for Cocoa Puff to feel safe enough to be turned out with the herd in our larger field.

Cocoa's first client sessions were "shadow sessions." I call them shadow sessions because clients had strict rules for interacting with her. Cocoa was in the arena, but she was not to be touched unless she touched the client first. She was not to be haltered or have any object put on her because she was in the arena to learn that other humans were safe. I wanted her to have freedom to move at liberty and choose to engage with other beings or not. She was there to learn from her fellow horses about how to build a relationship with humans. For a long time, Cocoa was like a shadow, not fully participating as a partner with clients. Finally, one day, she agreed humans were safe and stepped willingly into her role as an equine therapist. Cocoa excels in her role now and is typically drawn to clients who are in the process of healing pain and deep hurt.

Ashley, Cami, Barbara, and I entered the field, and all the horses lifted their heads. As we walked forward, a couple of them moved toward us, but Cocoa was the only one that closed the distance all the way to Ashley. We trust our horses to make safe and compassionate decisions for themselves as to whether they want to build a relationship with a new client. Cocoa seemed to be responding to something about

Ashley that drew her near. The pony walked toward us in a slow but steady fashion. As she approached, Ashley ducked in behind me.

"What is she doing?" Ashley yelled at me. Her eyes were open wide, her thick glasses making them look even bigger. She grabbed my arm and hid all the way behind me, peering out around me. Her eyes were glued on Cocoa. "Why is she coming so close?"

"Well, let's look at her, and maybe we can figure it out. Can you help me?"

Ashley nodded yes. Cocoa stopped about 3 feet away. Her ears were flicking back and forth rapidly. She sniffed with her nose outstretched toward us.

"When you meet someone new, like today when you met Cami and me, what does your body look like?" I asked.

"I don't know. I don't think I do anything different. Maybe I'm shy. Is she shy? Is that why she is sniffing her nose like that?"

"It could be. If she is a little shy, like you, how can we help her feel better?"

Ashley started to move out from behind me. Still holding on to my arm she whispered, "I could tell her I'm nice." She looked at Cocoa and shouted, "Hey, I'm nice!"

Cocoa snapped her neck back, threw her head up in the air, and snorted. She was getting ready to turn and walk away and Ashley added, "Sorry, I yelled. I'm nervous. But I am nice." She reached her arm out in front of her. She then moved her palm up so that it was facing Cocoa, in the same stop motion a crossing guard would make to oncoming traffic. It was an interesting clash of messages: *Come closer, no, stop.* Cocoa stopped her backward movement in response to Ashley's request. Ashley moved the rest of the way out from behind me. She was now standing in front of me closer to Cocoa.

The other horses in the paddock had resumed their normal behaviors by this point. A couple of them were munching hay, another was walking over to the water trough. Hook settled down for an afternoon nap. The ponies had silently agreed that Cocoa was taking the lead with our new client. Cocoa moved one step closer to Ashley, matching her movements. Cami and I looked at Barbara with smiles across our faces. We were encouraged to see the interaction Ashley had just had with Cocoa. Ashley had realized that her actions scared the pony. Not only did she take ownership of her actions, she was trying to fix it by apologizing. Barbara looked back and gave us a thumbs up.

We were getting close to the end of the hour session. I needed to find a stopping place. "I think Cocoa liked you letting her know that you didn't mean to scare her. Maybe she is a little bit nervous, too." I smiled and looked toward the little mare. "So we are out of time today. Do you want to tell her anything else? Also, do you want to work with Cocoa again?"

Ashley turned and looked at me and put her hands on her hips. "Duh!" she said. "Of course I will work with her next week. She is my friend." Turning back to Cocoa she waved goodbye. Ashley's whole body moved in the wave motion. Little for her was halfway; it was all or nothing. This would be a pattern we would see show up over and over during her time with us. "Bye, Cocoa! See you next week."

"Okay, sounds good," I replied. "Hey, I almost forgot: Before you leave, do you mind helping me pick up the crayons off the table so our office is clean and ready for the next client?"

Ashley was all smiles. "Sure, I like helping!" Off she went, literally skipping across the arena toward the office. She beat us all there and waited for me to catch up and open the door. We all picked up the crayons together. Ashley freely chatted, telling us about her favorite colors.

"Thanks!" I praised her. "We will see you next week. Maybe Cocoa has a favorite color you can ask her about when you see her again."

Ashley grabbed Barbara's hand and pulled her out the door.

We learned a few things from the first session with Ashley. Cocoa was willing to greet Ashley, giving us a clue that she wasn't an aggressive child who might be a threat. Ashley's approach seemed to be cautious but curious with Cocoa. The girl's impulse control could use a boost. Her awareness of where her body was in space and time appeared to be an issue for her, as seen in her struggle with objects, such as the door, or the table, and in the way she hurled herself into an area. We surmised that her *proprioceptive pathways* (which help you know where your body is in space and time) needed strengthening. Like many youngsters with attachment issues, she took my initial directions and requests as a threat. Given time and a chance to "fix things," she could, and appeared to even want to. We were encouraged by her ability to adapt to the input around her. Still, Ashley was going to be a complicated case because she was so quick to rely on her ingrained fight/flight/freeze reactions. We realized that if we were going to encourage her to make different choices about how she interacted with others, we needed to improve her self-awareness, so she could cope with someone other than herself.

Learning to Regulate Fight/Flight/Freeze Mode

We decided to start with Ashley on basic executive functioning skills to earn her trust and let her body and mind feel safe at the barn. We knew we couldn't do anything with her until she was out of defense mode and felt safe with us and the horses. Cocoa was to be her teacher and partner to start with. We kept the same routine every week to provide the structure she needed. We have found that many times people don't realize what structure is doing for them and why it works. It is simple—it allows you to be able to predict, say, 93 percent of the time, what is going to happen. (We like to leave a few percentage points for the "oops, just life" factors.) When our brain can predict a pattern for something, or someone, it deems that thing or person trustworthy. That is how basic trust is built. It is also how trust is broken and eroded. In Ashley's early development, her mind had no way of predicting what was going to happen to her. She didn't know when and where pain was going to come from. Her parents, the people who were supposed to keep her safe, were not predictable in their behaviors and treatment toward her and her siblings. If she cried or had a need, the response she got was apparently extreme and painful. Her mind struggled to make sense of it all. Being locked in small spaces for days on end taught her that having a need, physical or emotional, was useless. The one thing she could trust or predict was that humans were not something she wanted to interact with.

Once Ashley had been removed from her early home environment, her aggressive behaviors started to escalate. Why? She was in a safe place, and the adoptive mother was loving and caring. She knew what Ashley and her sister had been through and was trying to shower them with affection to make up for the first years of their life. She not only met the basic needs of the girls, she tried to give them the things they didn't have before: nice clothes, lots of toys, trips, and eating out. She gave Ashley her own room with all the beautiful "little girl things" she could want. So what drove Ashley to try to stab her adoptive mother and yell that she wanted Kari dead?

The simple answer was, *Ashley didn't know how to trust.* The girl's mind had developed by swimming in toxic levels of cortisol, adrenaline, and other stress hormones. When her brain should have been developing neuropathways for fine and gross motors skills, with her body giving her input about where she was in time and space, instead, her brain "cropped" those pathways because they were not being used. In fact, the input she was getting from her body was terror, and the natural result was that her developing mind eliminated that line of communication so she didn't have to focus on constant pain. Kari, her adoptive mom, with the best of intentions, was unknowingly triggering Ashley repeatedly into fight, flight, and freeze mode every time she expressed or asked about love. Ashley had no pathway for love; she only knew the language and feeling of fear.

Our plan was to help Ashley's body and mind come out of full fight/flight/freeze mode through consistent structure. The structure would slowly start to allow Ashley's body to be less guarded, because she would be able to predict what our sessions would look like. Cami and I also had to be predictable and trustworthy—we had to say precisely what we meant, not leaving anything to chance, at least at first. As her trust increased we would attend to the second stage of attachment and start to shift things around. However, before then we needed to remain consistent. As the equine person on our team, my voice was the lead on creating and holding the structure in the beginning. Cami was then free to focus on building rapport with Ashley. Ironically, Ashley instantly did not like Cami after we identified her as the therapist. The reaction was to be expected. When we first introduced ourselves, Ashley scowled at Cami, rolled her eyes as only a scornful adolescent can do, and shifted her body away from Cami and toward Barbara. The next time Ashley came to a session, Cami tried to greet her first, but Ashley stuck her tongue out at her and said she didn't need a therapist. Our strategy was to always include Cami in every reference and conversation so that while Ashley didn't have to engage with her, we did.

For example, during one of her early sessions, Barbara brought Ashley into the office. As Ashley ran into my office, our session began.

"What horse are we working with today? I want Cocoa again!"

I smiled at her. "Okay, I need to save this email. Can you go wait with Barbara and Cami? I will be right there." I turned around, back to my computer. A few moments later I walked out to the table, saying, "Thanks for waiting. That was very helpful. Now, on to you! How have you been since we saw you last?"

"I'm good. Can we go out now?"

"Well, not quite yet. Remember, first we need to catch up on the week. Can you tell Cami and me at least one good thing, and then maybe if you had any bumps in the road—the not-so-good stuff—since last week?"

"Today was okay. There is a guy that I like at school. I'm mad at my foster parents. They made me sweep the floor. I didn't want to do it, but I did. I get to see Mom this weekend. Good?"

Cami followed up, asking, "So there is a guy that you like? What is he like?"

The flow of the conversation helped us smooth over the fact that we were deliberately including someone Ashley didn't want to acknowledge (Cami), and Ashley answered naturally, blushing and smiling. "He is like me. He just got out of residential, too. He threatened a teacher but doesn't do that stuff anymore."

Cami nodded her head up and down slowly. "Wow, okay. Well, that sounds exciting, then. So when you didn't want to sweep the floor, and you got mad at your foster mom, what did that look like?"

"I yelled and stomped outside. I didn't hit or kick anyone. After a bit I came back inside and did it. I wanted to see my mom and I wasn't going to be able to if I didn't sweep the kitchen."

"Okay, so you fixed it," said Cami. "Good job! You get to see your mom. Do you know what you are doing with her on your visit?"

"We are going to meet at McDonalds for a treat with my sister. I'm going to get an ice cream cone!"

"Sounds like fun." Cami smiled and looked at me. The check-in was complete. It was our goal to keep the check-in modest. We didn't want to confront the girl with too much talk up front. Getting her to speak naturally with Cami was progress. Later there might be opportunities to ask more questions, but we needed to build a stronger level of trust and respect before then.

Cheerfully, I announced, "Okay! Let's go see Cocoa." Ashley was so excited she nearly fell over herself getting up from the table.

Cocoa was waiting in the arena along with our other ponies, Cookie and Squire. Ashley walked up to Cocoa and waited for her to say hello to her. Cocoa reach out her nose and sniffed Ashley's hand. Ashley reached up and petted her face and stroked her mane. Then turned to us. "What are we doing today?"

I looked around the arena. "Well, I've been teaching Cocoa how to walk through an obstacle course. She has been practicing walking over poles, around cones, making circles around barrels, stopping with a foot in the hula-hoop—stuff like that. Would you like to help me train her so she can know that it is okay to do those same sort of things with other people and not just me?"

"Sure, but I don't see a course here."

"Well, first we need to build one. Can you help me?"

"I guess." Ashley put her hands in her pockets and looked down at the ground.

Her response was less than enthusiastic with even a hint of resistance in her body as she looked away from Cocoa and me, and gazed at the ground. I made the choice to not respond and instead moved on.

"Great, thanks!" I said with an overly merry voice. "Okay, first we need to come up with what we are going to use. There are tons of different objects and materials in the arena. Would you like to build the course on your own or do you want me to help?"

My shift in tone transferred to Ashley. She changed her face to a smile and looked at me, saying, "I can do it." With that, she ran to the far corner of the area where we keep our "props." There were poles, jump standards, big black plastic barrels, diving rings, traffic cones of every shape and size, balls in every size, random stuffed animals and toys, hula hoops—pretty much anything you would want for imaginative play—along with "horsey stuff," like grooming tools, halters, and lead ropes. Ashley spent the next 10 minutes just going through things. Cocoa meandered down to the same corner and stood at Ashley's side as she searched through the items. A couple of times Cocoa reached in the toy box and came up with a stuffed animal in her mouth. She would shake and wave it in the air (photo 13). Ashley laughed and tried to take the toy from her, but Cocoa wasn't about to give up her prize! She appeared to be trying to play tug of war with Ashley, but the girl didn't want to play back and turned away to continue her search.

Ashley eventually picked up a couple of small diving rings and the sandbox tool toys—a little shovel and some molds for sand-castle-making. Cocoa was still interested in Ashley and followed her to the middle of the ring. Ashley smiled over at us. "She likes these things. Cocoa can make a circle around the ring, and she can pick up the shovel and help me build a sand castle." She had certainty in her voice as she shared what Cocoa was supposed to do in her project.

It wasn't likely that Cocoa was going to pick up the shovel and build a sand castle, but I made the choice to let it play out to see if Ashley could be flexible with her plan and adjust once she saw some difficulties with it.

"Okay," I said. "Just remember that Cocoa is big. Do you need any help with anything or do you have any questions?"

"No, I don't need help!" Ashley said with confidence. "Come on, Cocoa, let's go." She then turned and walked about 20 feet from Cami and me. Cocoa willingly followed and stopped when Ashley did. Ashley had about 30 minutes left in her session. I was curious to see what she would do with her items. She set down the diving ring first then walked about 3 feet from it and set down the sandbox toys. Ashley called to Cocoa, "Come on, Cocoa, come on." She patted her knees like calling a dog. "Cocoa, come on, make a circle. You can do it, come on, Cocoa."

Cocoa didn't move, but she did watch her. Cookie and Squire went to the other end of the arena and laid down for their afternoon nap. Ashley looked around then walked over to the sandbox toys. She sat down and started to dig in the footing with the shovel. Our arena has what is called "blue stone dust." It is like beach sand but made out of crushed stone instead, so it doesn't pack and hold the shape like beach sand would. Ashley filled up the first little mold—a wall piece. She flipped it over and pulled it up. The stone dust stayed somewhat in a shape but the little pillars at the top just crumbled and fell down. Ashley pushed the whole wall over and started again. After about three tries she stopped using the mold and just starting mounding up the footing into a hill. She shoveled and patted the hill. She pushed with her hand and moved more footing around.

After about 10 minutes of watching Ashley, Cocoa ambled over to her. Her nose was almost touching the ground as she walked. As Cocoa blew out her breath, little puffs of blue stone dust rose around her. Ashley didn't seem to notice Cocoa coming to join her. She remained fixed on shoveling and moving the stone dust into a large hill shape. Cocoa stopped less than a foot from her. She pawed at the ground near the spot where Ashley was digging. Some clients might have seen that Cocoa was trying to help, using her hoof as a shovel. Ashley did not acknowledge Cocoa with even a glance. Cocoa pawed at the ground again. Nothing. Cocoa then let out a loud sneeze. Ashley jumped and screamed in surprise. She picked up the shovel and threw it at the pony. Cocoa lurched backward and ran to join Cookie and Squire at the other end of the arena. Ashley immediately went back to digging in the footing as if nothing had happened.

Cami, Barbara, and I looked at each other. Ashley had just gone from startled, to aggressive, and back to her task in a matter of seconds. Nowhere in that cycle did she turn to us. Typically, if a horse scares a client, the next thing that happens is the client asks what happened or why the horse acted that way, or the client wants to share and process the fear. Nothing like that happened with Ashley. Her world remained just that—her world. She had a threat, she responded to the threat, and then moved on.

After a few minutes I said, "Hey, Ashley? Our time is almost up for this week. Can we check in on how things went out there today?" Ashley ignored me. Needing to wrap up the session, I walked just a little bit closer to her and repeated, "Ashley, sorry, but we are out of time. You can keep building the obstacle course next week. Can you come over and check in with Cami and me?"

Ashley exploded! "I'm not done. Can't you see I'm working? Why didn't you tell me that I was out of time? Why are you yelling at me? I'm not stupid, you know! What is wrong with you?"

Breaking Through

The tirade went on and on. There was no opening for Cami, Barbara, or me to speak. We let it be. Ashley stomped around the arena, kicked the mound of footing she had been working on, and threw another toy out into the middle of the arena. I couldn't even hear half the things she was yelling. After a few minutes the girl was exhausted, her body shaking. She collapsed onto a set of stairs in one corner of the arena that led to the office. Her face was streaked with gray dust and tears. Her glasses were sitting cock-eyed on her nose; her hands were filthy.

I had remained in the middle of the arena during Ashley's demonstration, waiting. I tipped my head to the side and asked, "Can you come over to Cami and me, or do you want us to come to you?"

Ashley looked up, huffed, then stood up and walked over to me. She put her hands on her hips. "Happy?" she snarled.

"Thank you, I appreciate you coming over to meet me." I took a long deep breath, resettling myself. The pause also gave Ashley's body a nonverbal cue to de-escalate, as well. "Okay, so, can you share what happened out there today with Cocoa?"

"She didn't want to play with me, so I played by myself." Ashley huffed again. Anger flashed across her face. "She got mad and decided to scare me. I didn't like it and told her to go away from me." She trained her eyes on me. "Then you yelled at me! You tricked me and didn't tell me I was out of time! So I don't like you!" She swung around so that she was facing away from all of us.

Even though I had not changed my tone or the volume of my voice, Ashley heard what I had said as "yelling." We soon learned that to her, when any sound or sensation broke through into her internal world, she took it to be an assault, and her response was to escalate. She believed I had tricked her and suspected I thought she was stupid for not getting the task we had discussed done. I did not believe that; however, in that moment I knew that if I tried to defend myself it would only enrage her again and give her something to push back against. We were still in the "forming trust" phase of our relationship. I chose to give her a sense of acknowledgment and set the foundation for learning not to worry if we did not get something done in a session.

"Wow," I began. "That sounds like a lot of things happened today. I'm sorry you are mad at me. I didn't intend to scare you or trick you. Unfortunately, it is my job to keep us on schedule. It is okay if we don't complete the activities each time. It is no big deal. We just pick up where we left off next week. Does that work?"

Ashley shifted her weight. She looked at Barbara. Barbara added, "Remember we are here to learn how to fix things. Michelle is trying to fix things with you. She didn't mean to scare you, and she said she was sorry. Do you want to fix things with Michelle or Cocoa?"

Barbara had been working with Ashley for six months, visiting her during her time at the residential program, and she had developed a trusting relationship with her. Therefore, Ashley was willing to follow her lead.

Ashley turned to slightly face me. Under her breath she said, "Okay, I can try again next week."

"Thank you for being willing. Now, I don't want to scare you next time I tell you we are out of time. Would it be helpful next week if I gave you an occasional update on where you are with time left during the session?"

"I guess." Then she added defiantly, "I didn't do anything wrong!"

This was the second time Ashley had become over-activated and agitated around doing something or being "wrong." It gave Cami and me a clue of where to focus some of our work. One of our treatment goals needed to be around the concept that it is okay to make a mistake and it is okay to try and fix things. Making a mistake or being wrong was sheer terror to Ashley. Barbara had disclosed that Ashley was frequently humiliated at school by her peers for her funny movements and bumping into things. To shield herself from potential hurt, anger had become part of her protective mechanism.

I shifted the topic. "Would you like to say goodbye to any of the horses or are you good?"

"I'm good. Cocoa was mean, and she hasn't fixed it so I'm not saying goodbye to her." This wasn't the time to push, so I closed the session. "Okay, we will see you next week."

Finding an Approach

Cami and I had just gathered more insight into how Ashley functioned in her world. She appeared to operate without time, losing track of even what was happening in her immediate environment when she was in her mental bubble. Ashley *could* fix things, but she had to release her energy before she could even look at entertaining repair.

If we were going to support Ashley as she learned how to refine her self-regulation, we had to start with helping her find her way out of "defense mode." Coming at her counterproductive behaviors head on was only going to drive her deeper into her protective patterns. We decided our approach was to use Ashley's perception that Cocoa had misbehaved. We could ask Ashley questions like, "What can we do to help teach Cocoa how to be nice? How can you teach her to trust? Do you have any ideas on how to help her learn to ask for attention without being mean?" If we could get Ashley to help us come up with a treatment

1. What we now understand is that animals gather their own insights about us and respond. This foal, Chloe, isn't far from her mama, and while she's nibbling on a stalk of grass, she is observing the photographer with an alert ear.

2. In this moment the two beings are connecting through eye contact and touch, a distinctly nonverbal flow of giving and receiving communication.

3. The wild horse has long been a cherished symbol of American freedom, and we see that same glorious heritage in our domesticated horses. Their nobility and beauty is part of what inspires us to draw closer and learn from them.

4. Today's horsemanship practices the subtle art of communicating with our horse partners without force or bullying, so that we can practice our own attunement with them. Michael is persuading Ruby to step back, and she's deciding how to respond.

5. Equine-Partnered Psychotherapy and Coaching relies upon the horse's honest response to a client. Communion with a horse creates a space for safety and hope, where trust is a two-way street.

6. For some people, horses with their long faces, big heavy feet, and powerful frames don't seem all that approachable or intelligible. Perhaps because they don't have eyebrows or faces that express emotion in the way we can read with dogs, horses have been mistaken as dumb beasts with no interior life, and therefore available for our exploitation.

7. As van der Volk comments, for some people, working with horses may be safer than dealing with human beings. This woman was apprehensive about working with horses. Bo tucked his head over her shoulder in a comforting embrace. His warm slow breaths filled her hand and warmed her chest, which in turn started to influence her physiology, encouraging her to slow down and bringing her body out of flight/fight/and freeze mode.

8. Week after week, Steve walked with Gypsy, talking to her, and working with her. While he was physically walking and talking with her, he was also walking with the pieces of himself he had lost in Vietnam, reclaiming them and giving those emotions a safe place to be felt, seen, and heard by another being.

9. "I had just turned thirteen that summer and was completely devoted to riding Schedule A."

10. Despite the awkwardness of the gate, Wastella recognized this child's need for connection. They stood together a long time, she nibbling gently on his neck, he with his face as close as he could get, and his hand caressing her cheek. Both were respectful with their requests for connection. This is exactly what happened for Michelle. She did not invade Schedule A's space; the intuitive horse immediately recognized her yearning for affirmation. It was the first time Michelle could recall being willingly touched since her illness.

11. "I had found what takes horsemen a lifetime to find—horses want connection and a relationship first and foremost." Michelle's bond with Diesel is the profound expression of the love that began with Schedule A, who taught her how much a relationship with a horse can be mutually beneficial and desired.

12. Cocoa Puff was slow to agree that humans could be trusted. She and Ashley had so much in common, we were not surprised that she was drawn to the little girl.

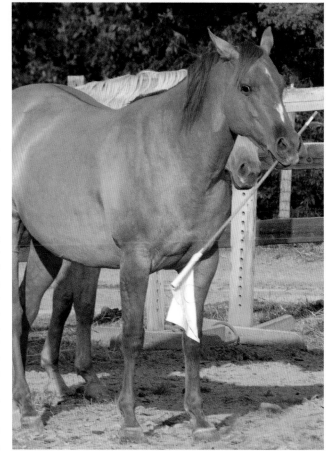

13. "A couple of times Cocoa reached in the toy box and came up with a stuffed animal in her mouth. She would shake and wave it in the air," much as Topaz is doing in her "capture the flag" moment here. The ability of the horse to engage with clients and the props they use is sometimes surprising to people, but horses can be curious and playful in EPPC sessions! They respond appropriately to the energy of the client.

14. Ashley was intrigued by Radar as he stood in the field by himself. "Did Radar understand what was happening? Did he think he did something wrong?" Her questions were perceptive and gave us some insight into how she was processing her own family situation.

15. This horse was hard to see as he was running around a shadowy indoor arena. And then he emerged, boiling up out of the dust and darkness. Radar's sudden appearance in Ashley's space must have been just as alarming to her.

16. Bo had a lot of encouragement from the group around him to go over this obstacle. Ashley was able to persuade Radar to accomplish a similar task but all on her own! Her success came because she and Radar had learned to communicate honestly and openly with each other.

17. Delilah's front half was refined and Arabian, while her hind end was strong and built for power. Her peculiar balance physically could also reflect her sporadic behaviors emotionally—she tended to swing from happy-go-lucky, to dissociative and/or aggressive, but always yearned for connection. It was interesting to watch clients with similar behaviors be drawn to her power and strength.

18. When Cocoa watched Brenda with Delilah, her head and neck were relaxed, and she moved her lips and jaw in a licking and chewing fashion. Typically for horses this is a sign of acceptance and willingness to engage. Here Puzzle and Alicia are similarly communicating with quiet, almost imperceptible body language. Just by sharing the space, there is a connection of acceptance between them.

19. Wiscy (short for "Wisconsin") was pretty, but he was also the baby on the property and still learning about personal space.

20. The other horses weren't that happy to have Wiscy on the scene. Here Peppy is trying to ask Wiscy to leave the hay manger, but Wiscy is not yielding to his request. With people, Wiscy brought the same energy. He became pushy with his enormous head, trying to get others to interact with him and meet his needs on his terms.

plan for Cocoa, and help us put that treatment plan into action, then she would, in essence, work her own treatment plan at the same time she was helping Cocoa. Everything that Ashley currently imputed to Cocoa was actually Ashley's projection of her own thought patterns. By turning the story over to Ashley, we would empower her with the ability to grow her own understanding and pathways for trust and respect.

After check-in the following week, I asked Ashley to say "hello" to the horses. She apparently was still holding a grudge: She looked at Cocoa first, chose to ignore her, and went instead to try and say hello to Cookie and Squire.

Walking over toward Squire, she said, "Hi, little guy. You are nice, aren't you? You're not like Cocoa, are you?" Squire tossed his head out to the side, made a large circle in the air with his nose, and snorted. He wasn't interested in what this girl was peddling! Ashley was startled by his response and jumped back. "Well, I don't like you either!" she yelled, and turned her attention to Cookie.

Cookie was a little dark-gray-and-brownish pony. He was a Shetland crossed with a Miniature Horse, so his proportions were a little off: His head was a bit large for his body, and he had a very round pony belly that wobbled from side to side as he walked. Cookie also only had one eye. I had selected these ponies to be in Ashley's sessions for specific reasons. Squire was playful and loved to have fun. Cookie, though, was standoffish and a little skittish, especially if someone was on his blind side. I had all the "pieces" of Ashley that we had seen up to this point represented in equine form: Cocoa for her willingness to connect, Squire for playfulness, and Cookie for his reactiveness. All three were masters at supporting clients when clients tapped into their feelings.

Like Squire, Cookie wasn't having anything to do with Ashley. Before she could even get close to him, he took off at a fast trot to the other end of the arena. Squire followed right on his heels. That left only Cocoa, who was looking directly at Ashley. Ashley looked back at

Cocoa as if thinking about her options. She looked down in the direction of Squire and Cookie. Then she came back to us with a scowl on her face.

"So, how did saying hello go today?" I asked with a slight level of concern in my voice to match her facial expression.

"Not good. They don't like me."

Scratching the side of my face, I gave my best impression of someone in deep thought. "Hmmm, I'm curious. How do you know they don't like you? What did they do to show you that?"

"Well, they didn't say hello, duh." Ashley waited for my next apparently dumb question.

I had one. "Oh, I see. Did they all not say hello, even Cocoa?"

"No, I'm mad at her because she was mean to me. So I didn't say hello to her."

Cami asked, "Is that something you typically do if you are mad at people, not talk to them?"

"Yeah, don't you?" Ashley rolled her eyes. "I get in trouble if I yell at them so I just don't talk to them."

Ashley looked at Cocoa, who had silently closed the distance from the far end of the arena toward us. Ashley's eyes got big and she pointed at the mare. "See, she is doing it again. She is sneaking up on us!" Ashley retreated backward toward the edge of the arena, away from Cocoa.

Cocoa stopped walking. Her head shot straight up in the air. Her ears flicked rapidly back and forth, and she was wringing her tail, all equine signs of being on alert. I had a chance to put our plan in motion.

"Wow, you are right! She did sneak up here. Look at her now. What does her body look like?" Once again I put on my best "thinking face" and raised my brows when I turned to look at Ashley.

"Well, now she looks scared because I caught her." Ashley seemed proud of herself. She stopped backing up and instead moved to stand next to me. "See, she is trying to decide what to do next."

"Hmmm, you're right again! So what should *we* do next? If, like Barbara said last week, we are here to learn how to fix things, is there a way we can help teach Cocoa to fix things?" I looked between Barbara and Cocoa, and then settled my eyes on Ashley.

"I don't know; she doesn't look like she is sorry. You can't fix things if you are not sorry. Well, I mean, you can, but people know you don't mean it, and it doesn't work."

As if on cue, Cocoa immediately lowered her head, looking almost pitiful. Her head was hanging below her shoulders, and she peered up at us with her large brown eyes. She stopped swishing her tail, and her ears dropped loose, hanging out to the side. "Hmmm, what does she look like now that you told her she doesn't look sorry?"

"She is just trying to butter me up," Ashley stated matter-of-factly.

"Is it working?"

This time it was Ashley who moved closer to Cocoa to close the gap. "Well, I guess so. I could tell her I don't like people sneaking up on me and not to do it again." Without prompting the girl walked over to Cocoa, leaned over, and shook her finger in the pony's face. "I don't like it when you sneak up on me. That is bad! Don't do it again." Ashley straightened up and placed her hands on her hips. Cocoa dropped her head even lower.

"Do you think she understood you?" I asked.

"Yes, she is sorry now." Reaching out, Ashley petted Cocoa's head. "Okay, I know you are sorry." She scratched the horse behind her ear. Cocoa leaned into the touch and stretched her neck out to let Ashley dig a little deeper.

"Okay, Miss Ashley, you asked me to let you know about time earlier during our session. You have only about 15 minutes left. What do you think would be a good way to spend what's left?"

"I think I need to be nice to Cocoa for a bit since she said she was sorry. What can I do with her?"

"Well, she seems to be enjoying you scratching her. Do you want to brush her?"

"Sure. How do you brush a horse?" Ashley lifted her head to look at me while scratching Cocoa's neck.

I walked over and picked up a little blue shower tote that we had turned into a groom box; it held all kinds of brushes. They all had different functions, but I didn't intend to give Ashley a lesson on proper grooming technique. What I cared about was letting her continue to explore her relationship with Cocoa.

"Well these are some of our brushes. Why don't you see which ones Cocoa likes? Also, you can see if she has any favorite places to be groomed." I placed the groom box on the ground close to Ashley and Cocoa and backed away to join Cami and Barbara.

A Moment of Connection

Cocoa is typically a little finicky with grooming. Some days she loves it and doesn't want to stop, while others she whirls away and takes off to the other side of the arena or pasture. I wasn't sure which Cocoa was going to show up today. I hoped it would be the one that liked being groomed. Ashley went to the box and started to explore the brushes. She picked up a purple hard-bristled brush first. She tested the brush on her hand and frowned. She dropped it back in the box and selected a small purple face brush. The face brush was very soft and fit in the palm of her hand. After testing it on herself, Ashley seemed to like it enough to try it on Cocoa. As the girl approached the mare with her arm outstretched, lurching and unbalanced, Cocoa raised her head in alert and started backing up.

"It's okay, it's okay," said Ashley in a soft consoling voice that we hadn't heard her use before. "I'm not going to hurt you. I just want to brush you." Cocoa stopped going backward but wasn't quite ready to agree to Ashley's proposal. The horse's ears were flicking back and forth, and she turned her head to the side, looking out into the open arena. I couldn't help but recall the similar movements Ashley had shown on her first meeting with us. She, too, had looked around and sized up her options and exit strategies.

Ashley noticed the questions coming from Cocoa as well. "Really, it's okay. I tried the brush first. It is soft, see..." She put her other arm up in the air next to the outstretched hand that held the brush and again brushed her palm with it. Cocoa, turned to look back at Ashley and pushed her nose out to sniff the air closer to the girl. "It's okay," Ashley repeated. "It's okay..."

Cocoa agreed. She walked over to Ashley and sniffed her hand and the brush. She then moved into Ashley, placing her head gently against Ashley's chest. Ashley froze. She didn't move to brush the horse, but she didn't retreat either. I held my breath, waiting to see what Ashley would do with what was a clear request from Cocoa to make a connection. Cocoa waited for a couple of seconds, too. Then, very gently, she nuzzled Ashley's body by moving her nose softly back and forth. Ashley giggled. "That tickles!" she said as she softly stepped to the side of Cocoa's neck and started to brush her. After a few strokes, the girl gave the horse an awkward hug, reaching her arms around Cocoa's neck. Cocoa returned the hug by moving her neck around Ashley's body in a "U" shape. Ashley whispered, "Bye, girl. I'll see you next week."

Ashley let go of Cocoa and walked back over to the groom box, dropping the brush into it. Cami and I had been quietly discussing whether or not to check in and process or debrief the session like we typically would. We decided not to, unless Ashley opened the conversation herself. We wanted to allow the connection between her and Cocoa to be the last thing Ashley experienced that day. If we tried to process it, we might shift her focus from the experience itself to talking about it. While we wanted Ashley empowered to trust language and sharing with other humans, she also needed to learn how to simply embrace the bodily connection and feelings she was having with Cocoa. Wordless, physical reconnections are as powerful, if not sometimes more powerful, then spoken insights in Equine-Partnered Psychotherapy. Accepting bodily contact with Cocoa was, at its core, accepting another form of trust. If we encouraged Ashley to talk about what had happened, it might distance her from the "felt body" experience she'd just had.

Ashley was all smiles. "I think Cocoa and I are friends again. She listened to me. I told her I'll see her next week."

Cami and I smiled at each other, and I said, "Good deal, we'll see you next week, too!"

Radar

Ashley's sessions went on in a very similar fashion for the next couple of months. She and Cocoa worked up to being able to make it through obstacle courses together. Ashley would explode from time to time, especially if she thought she did something "wrong" or she didn't get an activity done quickly enough. And Cocoa provided her own challenges: In some sessions the mare was willing, trusting, and patient with Ashley. At other times, Ashley spent the hour just trying to get close enough to the horse to say hello or put a halter on her.

After about 12 weeks Ashley had learned to consistently co-regulate herself in her relationship with Cocoa. She developed the skills, awareness, and language to be very clear with the mare what she wanted from their friendship. Her progress in the sessions seemed to be filtering to her life outside the arena, as well: Ashley was maintaining balance in her foster home.

But while Cocoa had become a trusted friend for Ashley and progress was being made with her foster care, the girl was still having some trouble in regard to reunification with her adoptive family. Her visits with her mom were okay as long as they were one on one, but Ashley was still showing trust anxiety when her sister participated and her mom's attention was split between the two siblings.

In thinking about how to address this lingering trust anxiety, we realized that Cocoa's story with us at Unbridled Change was potentially causing a block with Ashley. We had adopted Cocoa and she was at her "forever" home, and every time we tried to make a connection between Cocoa's journey and Ashley's, all Ashley could see and talk about was that we didn't "give Cocoa back" or send her away when things got rough. We had kept Cocoa and made it work. In Ashley's eyes, Kari, Ashley's adoptive mom, had not done that. As Ashley understood it, Kari had fostered her, adopted her, and then was "giving her back" to foster care because she was a bad kid. Nothing we said or did seemed to combat that line of thinking. And in truth, our saying it wasn't sufficient for Ashley. She needed to arrive at the understanding in her own words, in her own time. All we could do was continue to provide opportunities for her to find her own way to making sense of her world.

We had a new horse on the farm that was a free-lease with us for six months. His name was Radar, and he was a small, handsome, black Morgan-cross. He was built like a tank: about 14.2 hands but could hold an adult, so the perfect size for the mounted side of our program where we worked with rhythmic riding clients. We had just retired Frank, the draft horse that usually occupied this role, and we needed a horse to fill his spot while we searched for a suitable long-term replacement. Radar's owner was in her senior year of college and didn't have the time to spend with her horse. She wanted him to be well cared for and kept in light work—Unbridled Change was a perfect fit for both our needs.

We mentioned to Ashley we were bringing in a new horse to foster while his owner was finishing school, and she became very interested in Radar's story. She wanted to know why his owner would give him to us for a short time and why the owner was allowed to take him back if she was willing to give him up (photo 14). Did Radar understand what was happening? Or did he think he did something wrong? Her questions were perceptive and gave us some insight into how she was processing her own family situation. Ashley was getting closer to reunification with her adoptive family: They were beginning day visits where she had a chance to be home with her adoptive family, play, eat a meal, and then go back to her foster family.

Our fostering Radar was a perfect opportunity to explore the feelings Ashley had about being in foster care. Radar's "mom" couldn't give him what he needed right now, so his "mom" was trusting us to help him. Radar wasn't going to stay, though, no matter how much we liked him or he liked us. Eventually, when his mom was ready and able to be with him again, she was going to take him back home.

Cami and I asked Ashley if she would be willing to work with Radar to help him understand what was happening, and to explain that this was a safe place, just like she had with Cocoa. Ashley agreed, excited by the idea.

When Radar arrived, we placed him in our quarantine paddock for a couple of weeks for his and our other horses' safety. Ashley didn't realize that he was in the roadside paddock when she came into the office for that week's session. She was so eager, already yelling questions at me as she flung open the door, that she missed the threshold and tripped, lunging forward. Luckily, I was standing right there and caught her. Ashley didn't even acknowledge the trip or me holding her up, just looked up and shouted, "Where is Radar? Is he excited to meet me? Did you tell him about me?"

I flashed back to my first meeting with Ashley. I loved that her energy was so positive, and I was grateful that she was making eye contact, too. "Yes, he is here," I began. "You guys drove past him on your way in. Let's…"

Ashley cut me off: "Why is he out there? Can we go see him? Come on!" She turned and started heading back out the door. Cami, Barbara, and I agreed to skip the check-in—Ashley was on a mission!

Looking for a Way Out

As we walked across the parking lot, Ashley was looking in every direction. I realized that we had never brought her out to this paddock before. It was long and skinny, and ran along the edge of the road and up against the bank of a steep wooded hillside. The tree line created a dance of shadows across the grass.

Radar was standing next to the water trough in the shade of the wooded hillside, munching on grass. He had been in a boarding barn prior to coming to us so he was used to people coming and going. He picked up his head as we approached and flicked his ears a couple of times. He decided the grass was more worthy of his attention and promptly returned to grazing.

When we reached the four-board fence line, Ashley was still scanning every which way. "Where is he?" she asked frantically. "I don't see him! Did he run away?" An expression of terror and panic flashed across her face as she looked back at me. Radar was about 10 feet in front of her, eating with his head down and not moving. I wondered if she could see the black horse in the shadows. By this point I knew Ashley's triggers: If I pointed out Radar was right in front of her, she would be embarrassed, and typically, a meltdown followed. I didn't want the session to be swept up by that, so instead I called Radar's name, hoping that if he moved she would be able to see him.

"Raaaadaaaarrrr..." I called in a long drawn out voice, adding my whistle. Ashley had heard me call our other horses this way, and I hoped the familiar tone and cadence would help her nervous body calm down.

Radar jerked his head up and snorted, then walked over to the gate where we stood.

"There you are, Radar," I said. "Ashley was worried you had run away. Radar, meet Ashley." I reached my hand out for Radar to smell me and then motioned to Ashley to join me. Radar had to stretch his neck up high to get his nose over the four-board fence line. But he was tall enough that he wasn't able to lower his head to look at her with his head level through the boards. Instead, he had his jawbone resting on the top board of the fence, his nose stuck straight out toward us, and he looked at us from the bottom half of his eyes. He sniffed the air and tried to stretch a little bit more to reach Ashley's hand, which was farther away than mine. As he stretched, his large black nostrils flared even more. Ashley seemed unsure.

"Why were you hiding?" Ashley asked Radar in a shaming tone. "It is not nice to hide from people." Radar pulled his head in and lowered it to look at us through the open slots in between the wooden boards. He pawed at the ground with his front hoof and tossed his head up and down.

Ashley turned to me and asked, "Why is he alone?"

"Well, we put new horses by themselves for two reasons: The main reason is related to his health. We don't know if he has a cold or something else, so we give him a chance to settle from his trip while we make sure he isn't sick. That way he doesn't get all our other horses sick," I stated as I reached over the fence and petted Radar's face. "Once we know he isn't sick, then we slowly start to mix him in with one of the herds. Most likely our gelding herd—so Zane, Steel, and Doc."

Ashley watched the black Morgan. She moved to stand next to me at the fence. Her head just barely reached above the fence line, like Radar's. She placed both her hands on the top board, rested her head on top of them, and let out a sigh—a good sign that her body was starting to "come down" from the terror and panic she flashed just a few moments ago.

"So you are doing the same thing with him that you guys are doing with me and Mom," Ashley contemplated, "slowly putting us back together..." Her voice trailed off, and she looked tired at the thought. She leaned her whole body into the fence and sighed again. "I don't think he likes it. He doesn't want to be alone. Plus it is kinda mean because he can see all the other horses over there, but he can't be with them. Is he scared?"

I was surprised that Ashley made the connection so quickly. "I don't really know him well enough to say if he is scared or not," I stated, looking at Cami.

Cami followed my opening and asked Ashley, "Do *you* think he is scared?"

The young girl let herself hang backward off the fence with her arms outstretched and her hands gripping the board for support. She answered without looking at Cami, "Yes, because he doesn't know anyone." Radar turned and started to pace the fence line—back and forth he walked, from one end of the paddock to the other, his head lifted up so he could just see over the top board. "See, he isn't stopping. He was hiding and now he is looking around for a way out." Ashley stepped back, letting go of the fence rail.

Cami followed her lead and asked, "Have you ever felt that way?"

Ashley shifted her body toward the red gate to the paddock. Without looking at Cami she answered in a quiet voice, "Yes, I don't like being scared. I wished someone would help me when I was scared but no one ever did." Ashley stopped at the gate. She looked at me. "Can I touch him?"

I looked at Cami to see if she felt it was time for us to take this step. She indicated she did with a slight nod of her head.

"Sure," I said to Ashley, "if he will let you. But I need to go into the paddock with you to help keep both of you safe."

Ashley waited as I unlatched the gate. Radar stopped pacing as we approached him. Ashley stopped about 2 feet away and stretched out her hand for him to smell. "I'm here to help you," she told him quietly. "I know that you didn't mean to scare me when you were hiding. You were scared, too, not trying to be mean. Will you let me touch you?"

Radar pawed at the ground with his front hoof and tossed his head up and down slightly. He gave a little nicker. Ashley responded, "It's okay, it's okay. I'm not here to hurt you. I know you're scared. This is a nice place. We will take care of you. You just have to stay over here for a little bit more until she," Ashley pointed at me, "decides it is okay to let you meet some new friends. I had to be in a hospital for a while once, too, while doctors made sure I was okay before I could go to a new home and meet new people. So when you are ready, she will help you. I'll be here, too, and I can be your friend." Ashley moved a foot closer to Radar.

Radar mirrored Ashley's movement and walked a step toward her. He shook his head and nickered again. The girl reached out to pet his nose, and Radar let her, becoming still. While Radar was small for a horse, he was bigger than Cocoa in height and in overall size. Cocoa and the ponies were all very "light" horses in their body types. Radar was not. He had big bones and powerful muscles.

Ashley took all of him in with her eyes, saying, "He is bigger than I thought he was." She grinned at me as she stroked his neck.

I slowly nodded in agreement, smiling back at Ashley. "Yep, he looks small, but once you get next to him you realize he is a tank, not a small horse at all!"

Ashley and Radar stood with each other in silence for the next 10 minutes. Ashley petted him, and eventually Radar started to eat again. Ashley followed him, keeping one hand on him most of the time. In that time of silence, we saw Ashley regulate herself with a new horse. She was able to be in the moment with him, even after bringing up her painful past. She didn't get lost in her memories as she had done in previous therapy sessions. That day with Radar she was able to acknowledge being scared and make sense of it by explaining what she did to survive: hide and look for a way out. She also acknowledged what she wished for—someone to help her—and offered that to Radar.

Ashley ended the day telling Radar, "I am going to help you be okay.

I want to go back home, too, but we both need to be here right now because home isn't safe."

Something Wasn't Right

It just so happened that at the time Radar came to us, Ashley's home world had changed, too. The system placed another foster care child in her foster home—a boy about the same age as Ashley. Despite obvious progress in the arena with us, Ashley's behavior in the foster home and in school started to show regression. Her outbursts resumed. During visits with her adoptive family she would pick fights and threaten her mom and sister. However, in the arena with Radar, we watched a different story unfold. Radar proved to be the perfect new teacher for Ashley. He was patient with her and would stand perfectly still when she became overwhelmed by a task.

We were working with Ashley to build trust, as well as understand what it meant to be a "good friend." During one session in which Radar refused to move forward on her invitation, I asked, "What does a good friend do?"

Ashley squared up to Radar, put her hands on her hips and looked at him with annoyance. "Not this! He isn't listening to anything I ask! He isn't being a good friend." She then turned, walked away from him, and sat down on the ramp in the arena with Cami and me.

We sat there in silence for a few moments as Ashley huffed and slumped over with her head hanging in her hands.

Cami gently asked, "Well, if you don't like the way he is treating you, what do you want him to change?"

Still looking at the ground, Ashley replied, "I don't know…I want him to want to be with me. I don't think he wants to build trust with me. If he did, he wouldn't be mean and ignore me."

"Okay," said Cami, "you want him to change, but how do you ask him to change what he is doing from all the way over here?"

Radar was still standing next to a barrel at the far end of the arena where Ashley had left him. She had been trying to get him to walk in a circle around the barrel without a lead rope or halter. She had designated walking in the circle with Radar as symbolic of changing her behavior, but Radar had gotten halfway through the circle and stopped.

Just like where Ashley was in her treatment plan, Radar had only completed half the goal.

Radar picked up his head and looked at us, pawing at the ground. I commented, "I think Radar is trying to tell us something. He hasn't left the barrel, and now he is even pawing at the ground and looking at you." I watched Ashley squint in the horse's direction. "Can you see what Radar is doing there?" I asked.

Ashley shook her head no. We had suspected that Ashley's vision was worse than she was telling people, but this was the first time she acknowledged it.

"Can you see the shape of him?" I queried. Again she shook her head no. "Can you see him when you are closer to him?" Ashley shrugged her shoulders, so I followed up. "Does it scare you that you can't see him well?" Ashley didn't respond at first, then slowly she nodded her head yes.

Cami, Barbara, and I all looked at each other.

"Does your mom know that you cannot see that well even with your glasses on?" I asked her. Again a shake of the head. "Do you think you need to go to the doctor and get a new prescription?" Another shrug of the shoulders. Radar started to walk closer to us. The sound of his hooves walking through the crushed stone dust got her attention. I watched the girl scan the arena and noted that she didn't seem to locate the source of the sound. Radar stopped about 10 feet away from us, looking directly at Ashley. Ashley didn't respond to him. "Do you know where Radar is now?" I inquired.

"Yeah, he is down there by the barrel," Ashley said.

We realized that Radar's dark coat made him hard to see in the indoor arena (photo 15). The large black barrel was still down at the other end of the ring, but Radar was no longer there. Just then Radar let out a soft whinny and pawed at the ground. Ashley jumped in fright and surprise, almost falling off the ramp. Luckily Cami and I both reached out and grasped each of her arms, slowing her fall and giving her time to get her feet somewhat under her.

"He scared me on purpose!" she cried out. "He isn't a nice friend! He is trying to hurt me!"

Ashley was in full panic mode. Her eyes were wide, and for an instant, a look of terror came over her face. But the terror quickly turned to anger. "Why didn't you guys tell me he was right here? You tricked me, too! You *wanted* him to scare me! I hate you guys!" Ashley tried to run out of the arena, but at the gate she couldn't get the latch undone. Radar moved to stand next to the frantic girl. He reached out, ever so slightly touching her back with his nose. "Stop it!" Ashley screamed at him. Radar did not run away; he didn't even step back an inch. "I told you to stop hurting me!" Ashley shouted again. Radar stood still and the girl ran back to us, yelling, "He is hurting me and nobody is helping me!"

Calmly, Cami asked, "*Who* is hurting you?" We'd both had a feeling for a couple of weeks that something was not right in Ashley's world besides her eyesight. Every time we asked, Ashley was quick to say everything was fine, and she just wanted to get home. But neither Cami nor I thought she was talking about Radar at that moment. Cami asked again, gently, "Who is hurting you, Ashley?"

Ashley looked at Barbara, crying now. "My foster brother," she said through tears. "They tell him to punch me when I don't do something right." Radar shook his head up and down and pawed at the ground again where he stood. "I didn't think anyone would believe me...I'm not lying!"

We spent the next four hours with Ashley, working through what was happening. She threatened to run away if we told anyone else what she had shared with us. She refused to leave the barn, saying she wanted to sleep there with her friends. Eventually, a representative from the Department of Social Services arrived, and we were able to help Ashley tell her story again. Ashley was removed from her foster home, a child protection services case was opened, and she was placed in a different foster home with a family we knew well from past children they had in their care.

Ashley learned a new lesson that day with Radar: She didn't have to hide bad things. She had people and horses she could trust who would help her.

Ashley's behavior steadily improved after switching foster homes. She visited the eye doctor and received an updated prescription. While Radar remained hard for her to see when he was far away, Ashley changed her approach when she couldn't locate him. She began to ask, "What is he doing right now?" or "Is he over there or is that a barrel?" Ashley was learning to accept help and to be open to the answers we would give her. She was learning to trust.

Halfway

One of Ashley's last sessions with us is one of the most memorable I have had in the 17 years I have been in this field. She was facing one last big obstacle in returning home—whether she could trust her adoptive mom, Kari, again. Just as Kari needed to be able to trust Ashley, the young girl needed her adoptive mom to not hold the past against her. Ashley was at a point in her treatment where she understood that we couldn't *make* her mom trust her again—that was up to her mom. Ashley decided that the only person she had control over was herself. She decided that if she believed in herself and was willing to use the coping skills she had learned from the horses with others that her mom would be able to feel the difference, and would, therefore, trust her.

We asked Ashley to build an obstacle that represented this last big challenge to getting home. She could use anything in the arena to build the obstacle. Once it was constructed, her job was to ask Radar to accompany her through it. Ashley didn't hold back. She grabbed a large black tarp and stretched it out about 10 feet wide, leaving many folds and puffy spots that made it stand up off the ground. (For some horses this would already be a challenge—if they haven't been exposed to walking on a tarp, horses typically don't like putting their feet onto unidentifiable things.) Next she rolled two large, black barrels over to the tarp and laid them down on their sides—one on either end of the tarp. Radar watched as she made multiple trips to the prop corner of the arena and back to her obstacle, next dragging two white poles over and placing one end of each of the poles on each of the barrels. The poles created a small "x" over the tarp—what amounted to a low jump.

Ashley stood back and smiled.

"Are you done?" I asked.

"Yep, that looks pretty scary. If he trusts me to go over that then I'm a good friend."

"Okay, sounds like a good plan. Do you need anything else from us?" I queried.

"No, I'm good."

With that Ashley turned to greet Radar. They said hello, and then the horse followed her over to the jump. I thought Radar would step over the jump quickly due to his background in the sport of eventing, which involves galloping cross-country over fences. He had been trained to go over imposing obstacles like they were no big deal. But I was delighted to watch Radar forget about all his training and instead respond to what Ashley believed the obstacle was: *scary.*

Radar got up right next to the jump and stopped. He tossed his head back and started to back up with a wide, scared eye. Ashley responded to his behaviors of fear with quiet words. "It's okay, it's okay…" she said softly, petting the side of his neck. "I know you are scared, but I'm going to help you. See, it is no big deal." Ashley reached over and touched a pole. Radar stopped backing up but kept shaking his head up and down. He pawed at the tarp. The tarp moved under his hoof and the horse shot backward again.

"Whoa, it's okay," Ashley said a little more loudly. Radar stopped and lowered his head to the ground, pawing at the stone dust. The girl came up to him and stroked his neck again. "I know: If I go first, you will see that it is okay." Ashley took off at a run and leaped at the jump. Cami and I held our breath because we were not so sure she was going to make it over without falling. But she did it! Once on the other side of the obstacle, she yelled back to Radar, "See, I'm okay! You can do it, too!" Ashley motioned with her arms for him to come to her and patted her legs. "Come on, Radar, you can do it! Come on!"

Radar looked around the arena. I thought he seemed to be weighing his options. He chose to move closer to Ashley and the obstacle. He walked straight up to the jump, stopping just in front of it again. He stretched his neck out as far as it would go toward Ashley's hand on the other side, and she softly touched his nose.

"That's right, come on, you can do it. You can trust me," she urged. Radar picked up his right front leg, and I thought he was going to step over. Ashley thought so, too. "Yes, that's right, good job!"

Radar's hoof hit the pole, and it rolled off the barrel. Radar jerked his leg back and pawed at the pole that was now lying flat on the tarp on the ground. Cami and I thought Ashley would leave the pole where it had fallen, based on her past actions. Previously, if a horse moved or knocked something over in a course she would justify the change and not fix it. This time, though, she surprised us.

Ashley reached down and put the white pole back up on the barrel, saying, "It's okay, you didn't mean to do that. I can fix it. See, no big deal." Then the girl turned back to Radar. "Watch me do it again." Ashley stepped over the poles. Then she did it again. Back and forth she went, over the small jump, talking to Radar the entire time. She encouraged him with all the same phrases we had used over the past months to encourage her—she had not only heard them, she had understood them and could use them with her friend. Radar repeated his pattern of backing up, coming back, lifting a hoof, hitting a pole, and pulling back a few more times.

After about 20 minutes the pattern shifted: Radar placed his right front leg on the other side of the poles without hitting them. He was now standing in a very awkward position, staring at Ashley and waiting. Ashley, very excited with the gelding's new progress, praised him enthusiastically: "That's right! Good job. Now you need your other leg." She jumped back over the poles and tried to pick up Radar's left leg. The Morgan tried to shift his weight so he could do as she asked, but the motion pulled his right leg back toward him, and the poles started to fall. "Wait, wait!" Ashley called out. Reaching down to stabilize the poles, she let go of his leg, then yelled toward us, "If I let go of the poles they are going to fall! I can't help Radar and hold them up."

"You might be right," I replied. "Which one do you think will help Radar the most?"

The girl paused in thought, then said, "Maybe holding up the poles and cheering him on; that way they will not move and scare him again. Radar, I'm going to hold the poles. You can do this! Just pick up your other leg." The horse picked up his left leg and pulled it up and over the poles, placing it next to his right. Now he had his front legs over but his back legs were still on the other side of the jump. Ashley placed her hands on her hips. "Well, now what? You have to keep coming."

Radar disagreed. He relaxed his left hindquarter, cocked his leg, and closed his eyes. It appeared that he wanted a nap.

Ashley did not like this response. "What are you doing? You can't go to sleep now. You are halfway there. Come on! Wake up!" She reached up and gave his neck a pat with a bit more force then she'd used earlier. Radar's neck gently swayed with the rhythm of her touch. Still, there was no movement in his feet. Apparently the horse had a point to make.

"Why won't he move?" Ashley asked me in frustration.

"I don't know. There could be a lot of different reasons. What do you think?" I asked, throwing the question back to her.

"Maybe he's tired. Maybe he doesn't think he *can* move. I don't know. He is making me mad."

"I can see that." I smiled at the young girl. "In the past when Radar has gotten 'stuck' like this, it was his way to get you to talk about something. Is there something else you need to talk about that might be keeping you at 'halfway'?"

"I don't know." And then, "Maybe it is that I don't think Mom is ready for me to come home. I don't think she wants to trust me again, even after all the work I've done."

Unfortunately Ashley's intuition was correct. Her adoptive mom was struggling with whether or not she could have Ashley come back home. Not because she didn't love her, but because she was dealing with her own past and the trauma that Ashley's old behaviors had triggered in her. While Kari loved her adopted daughter, Kari couldn't separate the young girl from other people who had hurt and betrayed her in her own past. Ashley was ready to go home, but her mom was not in the same place. Although Kari hadn't shared this concern with Ashley, she had shared it with Social Services. Ashley could feel the division in her mom.

"Do you think your mom is scared like Radar was?" Cami asked.

"Yes, that is why he is stuck. Because I'm stuck. But what can I do if my mom doesn't want to trust me again?" Ashley looked down. Her body collapsed onto one of the barrels. Radar didn't move.

"Maybe your mom still has some work to do on her own," Cami went on. "Do you think you can give your mother some more time to work through being scared, even if that means not going home right away?"

Without moving his feet, Radar reached his head over and softly blew in Ashley's hair. He nuzzled her cheek with his muzzle.

"I don't know," the girl said quietly. "I just want to be home."

"We know that," Cami acknowledged, "but sometimes things take longer than we want. Sometimes we get mad like you did with Radar. But does that mean you don't want to be his friend?"

Radar nudged her with his nose a couple of times. Ashley stood up and stroked his neck.

"It's okay, I'm sorry, too." They stood together for a moment. Then Ashley said, "I get it now. I can only do half of this. The rest is up to my mom."

Radar stretched his neck up like a big bow and let out a loud sigh. He then took two steps and went over the rest of the jump (photo 16). On the other side, he turned and faced Ashley. He lowered his head into her chest, and the girl stroked his head. "Thank you, boy. You are a good horse. You just wanted me to see things. Thank you for trusting me." Ashley closed her eyes and leaned into the horse before her.

Radar and Cocoa had supported Ashley during a long and crucial transition in the attachment-trust dance. Cocoa had stepped up and volunteered to be connected with Ashley, sensing the great need emanating from her disjointed activity. With Cocoa, Ashley had a companion who gave her a chance to practice self-regulating without punishment. Radar put aside his training in order to accompany her as she faced her fears. He refused to move until she was ready to acknowledge what scared her; when she could say it out loud, he found his own release. The final sessions with Radar revealed to Ashley that she only had to be responsible for her own half.

What Came Next?

In the weeks following Ashley's breakthrough with Radar, Kari, her adoptive mother, decided she couldn't overcome her own trauma triggers. Kari asked to terminate her parental rights. Social Services and Ashley's caseworkers decided the best place to tell the young girl this news was at the barn surrounded by our horse-and-human support system.

Ashley was placed in a new residential facility that could support her as she coped with her adoptive mom's decision. Ashley wrote to us (and the horses) while at the facility, thanking us for helping her believe in herself, learning to trust, and coming to understand that she was worthy of love. Ashley thrived in her new environment, and she was soon placed in a loving foster family, which eventually turned into an adoptive forever home.

THREE

Delilah to Diesel: Taking off the Mask and Asking for Help

Brenda

"Brenda's" referral simply stated mental health issues surrounding PTS, a history of domestic violence, trauma, depression, and a bipolar diagnosis. Her goals for therapy were reunification with her children, who had been removed from her home because of domestic violence. While Cami and I tend to prefer not to have too much outside input before meeting a client, this wasn't much information, given that the referral goal was for reunification of a parent and her children.

Brenda walked into our office, her eyes blank and expressionless. She was an overweight woman with long blonde hair corralled with various bobby pins and clips. In a robotic voice she asked, "Is this Unbridled Change?"

Cami smiled, and answered, "Yes. Are you Brenda? I'm Cami. Nice to meet you. You can have a seat at the table, and Michelle and I will be right there."

Brenda quietly sat down and did not say anything else. Cami and I finished up our respective desk tasks and then joined her at the table. We started the intake process, explaining what Unbridled Change was, what could be expected from Equine-Partnered Psychotherapy, and why horses could help. We explained that we believed that Brenda had the answers for what was going to work best for her, and that our job was to help her find her way and her voice again.

Closed Down

Brenda sat still as a rock. Every time I paused and asked if she had any questions, she shook her head no. Her body language was closed: She sat square to the table with her arms folded over her chest. If she had been wearing a sign on her chest it would have read something like, "I don't want to be here, so fuck off!" I just kept smiling and going through the overview of horse safety and the rules of our program.

Cami took over when it was time to check in on treatment goals. "So, now that Michelle has told you about our program, I'd like to talk a little more about you and what you would like to work on while you are here. We don't have much information from Social Services, and since you are our client, can you share what you would like to accomplish?"

Brenda remained absolutely still. Her eyes moved from Cami to me. Slowly and with the same robotic voice, she said, "I want my kids back. They said I had to come. So here I am."

Cami nodded. "Okay, we can work on that. So…parenting skills?"

"Sure."

We both knew we were not going to get much more from Brenda that day, so we asked her to fill out the necessary paperwork. She went through each sheet mechanically. Her movements seemed detached. Her handwriting was neat. When she completed our intake forms, she put the pen down and looked at us.

As I reached over for the packet I asked, "Do you have any questions about our program, what you want to work on, anything at all? I know we threw a bunch of information at you." I smiled and tried to invite interaction on any level. I turned my gaze toward her and softened my posture to give her a sense of calm through my relaxed body.

In response, she stiffened and leaned back into her chair, away from the table.

"No. Am I free to go?"

"Sure, we will see you next week. We will be out with the horses after a quick check-in."

Brenda silently pushed her chair back, turned her eyes down, and walked out of the office. Cami and I looked at each other. We were not quite sure what to make of it. We couldn't tell if she was dissociating or if she was just pissed at the world. *Dissociation* happens when a person's system is on overload and the individual is in flight, fright, freeze, and/or faint mode. Brenda's robotic responses and faraway presence might have been signs of dissociating. In such a state, people typically stop responding to outside stimulus and detach from actively reading the world around them in order to survive the perceived threat. When working with horses, dissociation can be a huge safety issue because the client is not actively interacting with the environment. Instead the client tends to "hunker down" and the environment dictates what is going to happen. I was concerned that Brenda might be a little too dissociated to safely put her in with a horse. Was she "in the room" enough to respond to safety issues?

To help give us a little more insight into her level of connection to the outside world while also keeping safety in mind, I chose to start her with two of our mares: Delilah and Cocoa Puff.

Delilah

Delilah, a light gray (almost white) horse with specks of darker gray sprinkled all over her body (in "horsey terms" her color is known as "fleabitten gray") was an Oldenburg-Arabian cross that had been donated to our program. Typically this cross is sought after for its combination of refinement and speed from the Arabian crossed with the dynamic strength of the Warmblood. Unfortunately, Delilah's "mixing" did not turn out so proportional: Her front half was refined and Arabian, while her hind end was strong and built for power. The result was that, in movement, her hind end overwhelmed her front end and she was often thrown off balance (photo 17). Imagine a puppy that is still growing with a hind end bigger than his front end—when he starts to run, he almost flips over himself from lack of coordination. That is what Delilah looked like in motion. It wasn't uncommon for her to be cantering in the field, do a happy little neck roll, and almost fall over because her balance was so poor.

When I went to pick up Delilah from the donors, she was so dead set on not getting on the trailer it took me over an hour to load her. I was offered whips and ropes to try and force her on the trailer and speed the process along. Instead I let us approach loading at a slow and steady pace, gaining her trust, taking one step, then another, and so on until she willingly walked onto the trailer under her own power. I took my time that day because I knew it would set a precedent for her relationship with me.

Once at our farm, Delilah continued to follow her pattern for bracing for a fight with everything. However, you could tell she really yearned for connection and trust and that her "fight" was just a front. The mare also had an interesting behavior pattern in the field with our other horses. She would get a "dead" look to her eye, and oftentimes I would watch her stand in one spot for hours, not even trying to move. Her body was there but that was about it. If the other horses in the herd asked her to move, she did so as if she was dissociated from her body—her movements were mechanical-looking and listless. When Delilah "came back into her body," she would turn and run at any horse near her, without rhyme or reason, her head low and snaking out in front of her, her ears pinned so flat against her head you couldn't see them. She would even bare her teeth—and this was not a smile! She would use this display of aggressive body language until a horse totally submitted and turned away from her. Delilah didn't do this over food or for a spot in the shade. She just did it. And after running the other horse off, she would return to her dissociative state, checking out again.

In client sessions, you could sense and feel that every part of Delilah wanted to belong to someone, to be in partnership, but she made the client work for that connection and trust. She did not charge our clients when she felt overwhelmed. Instead she removed herself to the edges of the arena and watched them work with the other horses. The mare seemed attracted to clients with similar behaviors to hers. She would become very soft and almost mothering with them. It was as if she understood those clients had been taught to not think for themselves, to escape into their own minds, or to check out mentally from the here and now (dissociate). She seemed to know what they needed most was to be accepted.

In our short intake session my intuition said Brenda was someone Delilah would be attracted to. Like Cocoa Puff, she was drawn to clients that were hurting and afraid on the inside, no matter how aggressive, mad, mean, or sad they acted on the outside.

Nothing Moved

Delilah and Cocoa Puff were waiting in the arena. Brenda was early for her appointment, and since she was the first client of the day, we told her we could go ahead and start. She sat down in the same end seat at our table where she'd sat the week before. Cami and I found chairs on either side of her.

I began: "We typically like to do a quick check-in with our clients at the beginning of each session to see how the week was since we last saw you. It also gives you an opportunity to ask us any questions you might have had about the last session. If we gave you any 'homework'—something to reflect on or explore during the week—we might ask about that, too."

Brenda stared blankly back at me. She blinked maybe three times during my brief explanation. Her body language was still coming up "empty" for me—she wasn't giving me any signals that I could read. I looked at Cami.

"Do you have any questions or anything you would like to share or talk about before we go in with horses today?" Cami asked, raising her eyebrows and waiting for a response.

Brenda stated flatly, "No."

"Okay, well, just a quick reminder that you have the right to tell my horses, 'No.' You can do that by using the word, 'No,' and by making yourself—your body—big." I stretched my arms up in the air and out to the side to make my body look like a large capital "Y," then added, "And the horses have the right to tell you, 'No,' as well. They do that by moving away or refusing to move. What neither of you have is the right to cause harm to each other. If that looks like it is going to happen, I'll give you a heads up, at which time you or I can call a timeout and regroup. Any questions on that?"

"No."

With that answer, I stood up. "Okay, then, let's head on out into the arena and meet some horses." Smiling, I opened the door. My left arm made a sweeping "out" motion toward the arena, and I waited for Brenda and Cami to stand up and walk through, then closed the door behind them, took a deep breath, and said a little prayer that my horses would give me some insight as to where to go with this client.

Cami and Brenda waited at the wooden gate as I reached down and undid the chain that held it shut. As the chain clinked, both the mares perked their ears toward us and picked their heads up to look at us. Neither moved their feet to come greet the new visitor to their space.

We walked into the arena, and I closed and locked the gate behind us.

"So these are two of our four-legged team members," I explained to Brenda. "The grayish-white one is Delilah and the little tri-colored pony is Cocoa Puff. Our first day is simple and basic and designed to just give you a chance to get comfortable with the horses. We would like you to go and meet them, in whatever way works for you. Like when you meet a new person, you can see if you pick up something about their personalities. When you are done, feel free to come on back here to us. Remember, like we talked about last week, there is no right or wrong way of doing things as long as you follow three basic rules: One, you can go 98 percent of the way to the horses but they need to close the gap and touch you first. Two, do no harm—to yourself, the horse, or us (and the same rule applies for the horses). Three, you need to stay in the area where I am, since I'm the insurance that all is okay. Outside of those rules whatever works for you will work for us." I paused and looked out in the area to see if the horses had moved at all. Nope. "Oh, and if you need anything or have any questions, Cami and I are here, just ask."

Cami and I took a couple of steps back from Brenda to give her the space and nonverbal cue that she could move. Brenda did not move. She remained perfectly still with her eyes focused on a random point in space. We waited.

After a minute or so Cami said, "Do you need anything?" Brenda shook her head no. Cami added, "Okay, then, we will be over by the ramp if you need us or have a question."

I wasn't sure if Brenda understood our directions, so I added, "Feel free to move around if you want to approach a horse. It is up to you what 'Hello,' looks like."

Cami and I turned and walked over to lean against the ramp. For the next 25 minutes nothing moved in our arena. The horses didn't move, Brenda didn't move, we didn't move. Delilah cocked a leg and closed her eyes. Cocoa Puff remained alert. Her weight was evenly spread out between all four legs. Her head remained up and her eyes open. Her ears were trained on Brenda. She was facing Brenda but did not look directly at her.

After 25 minutes Brenda turned, looked at us, and asked, "Can I go?"

Cami said, "Sure. Do you need anything?"

"No. Can I go?"

"Yes," I replied this time. "We will see you next week." I opened the gate for her, and she walked to her car.

Cami and I still didn't know what our treatment plan needed to include or look like. Delilah had checked out with Brenda, but Cocoa didn't make a commitment one way or the other. She had remained frozen but focused on the blonde woman. The mares came up to me after Brenda left. Horses absorb the human emotions released during a therapy session, and I had developed a ritual to help "clear" any connection to what may have happened or emotions that weren't theirs. I thanked them both out loud and wiped them down with my hands, in a sense "giving them permission" to continue with their day as I led them back to their paddock.

Session Two

Brenda was early for her second session, too. She came into the office, sat in the same spot at the table, and told us she had no questions and nothing to share. I walked us back out to the arena where Delilah and Cocoa Puff were again waiting. We started with the same task: say hello to the horses, then come on back to us. I added this week, "Once you have said, 'Hello,' in whatever way is right for you, we are going to add the next step. Pick a horse and ask her to go to the cone in the middle of the ring and then come to Cami and me. Again, there is no right or wrong, and you can use anything in the arena as a resource to help you if you want." I pointed to the cone in the middle of the ring.

Delilah stood on the far end of the arena, past the cone, facing us.

Cocoa Puff was moving along the wall, her head down and her attention on looking for small pieces of hay that might be hidden somewhere in the footing. She was not watching us, nor did she acknowledge us as we came in.

Brenda remained still again, but this time, instead of staring into space, she looked right at Delilah. I'm not sure how long it took, but it felt longer than 10 minutes before Brenda started to walk across the arena toward the gray mare. Delilah did not move. Her eyes and ears remained locked on Brenda who closed the gap between herself and Delilah. Brenda stopped about 3 feet from the horse. Brenda didn't reach out her hand or make any overture toward Delilah. They stood that way for a few more minutes.

We noticed Brenda was swaying gently back and forth. She shifted her weight from her left foot and back again in a rhythmic motion. Her arms were crossed in front of her chest. Delilah matched Brenda, shifting her weight from one hind foot to the other, swaying her hind end gently back and forth. Cocoa Puff stopped looking for hay and turned to face the pair from the opposite end of the arena. We heard crying, but we couldn't see Brenda's face to confirm it was coming from her. Then we heard humming—the faint sounds of a tune. Delilah stopped shifting her weight and moved just a few small steps toward Brenda. Slowly the woman lowered one of her crossed arms to her side as she kept humming and swaying.

Delilah moved two more strides and stopped within a couple of inches of Brenda. She slowly lowered her head so it was even with Brenda's chest. The swaying and the humming continued. Delilah reached over and sniffed Brenda's dropped hand. Brenda stopped swaying and touched her back, brushing her hand against the tip of Delilah's nose. After the brief connection, they both drew back a step. Brenda returned to swaying and humming. Delilah closed her eyes, shifted her weight to one hind leg, and stood quietly.

After a few more minutes, Brenda turned and walked across the arena toward the gate. She stopped and looked at us almost pleadingly. "Can I go now?" she said. Tear marks streaked her face, and her jaw was trembling.

Cami asked, "Do you need anything?"

"No. Can I go now, please?"

Cami nodded to me so I walked over, unhooked the chain, and opened the gate. "We will see you next week," I said. Brenda had not chosen to share her experience with us, and we wanted to respect her privacy and honor her request.

Cami and I watched her walk to her car and exit the parking lot. We turned to each other, and I let out a sigh. "Well, we got some information," I said with relief. "Delilah wants to make a connection and Cocoa is curious. I guess we see what Brenda brings to the next session."

Cami agreed, adding, "*If* she comes back. I'm not sure she will."

"They Act Like I'm Not Around"

Brenda did come back. She was early again. She came into the office and sat down in the same chair. However, this time she did not look disconnected. This time her eyes already had tears in them. Her posture was not rigid but slumped over as if she was carrying a huge, heavy bag. Her arms were uncrossed, and she placed her forearms on the table and began wringing her hands.

Cami and I got a quick glance at each other and silently acknowledged the shift in Brenda's appearance.

Cami started. "I want to check in on last week before we go out. At the end of the last session, you looked like you had tears on your face, and I think we heard singing or humming coming from the other end of the arena. Do you want to share what was going on then? Or what is going on this morning? Because you look the same way now."

Brenda picked up her gaze from her hands and had the same

pleading look across her face. She looked at Cami, at me, and back at her hands. She spoke, but this time the voice that came out was shaky and full of emotion. "I was nervous." She paused and we waited. "I hum when I'm nervous; it helps me calm down."

"What were you nervous about?" Cami asked.

"I didn't know if you guys would be safe or not…if you would judge me like all the others." Brenda lifted up her eyes again and looked directly at Cami, and then me. "Everyone thinks I'm stupid. Everyone thinks I can't do anything because I'm bipolar. They talk to me like I can't understand them. I guess I thought you guys were going to be the same. But you weren't. You let me be. People don't do that. They judge me and act like I'm not around."

She looked down again and tears silently fell from her eyes and rolled down her cheeks. She started to hum again. We sat in silence with her. After a few minutes Brenda stopped humming.

I asked, "Is there anything you need from us that would be helpful?"

We ask this question a lot. We like it because it offers help but leaves the ball in the court of our clients to ask for it. That way, the clients have the chance to decide what is truly needed in that moment—sometimes it is outside help, but sometimes (most of the time) they just need permission to answer their own questions.

"I want to go say hi to Delilah again and try to get her to the cone. Can we go now?" asked Brenda in a shaky voice. Her body was braced for a no from us. She recoiled back into her chair, and her chest sank inward. Her arms moved back to a defensive position, crossed against her chest. Her words asked for permission for what she wanted, but her body was showing signs of not believing that asking for what she wanted was a good idea.

I smiled, stood up, and started to move toward the door, away from her to relieve pressure. "Sure—sounds like a good plan."

The horses had reset themselves as if by command, but we didn't stage them that way. Cocoa was along the left long side of the arena, nose-down again. Delilah was at the far end, past the cone. Brenda walked into the arena. She stopped for a second and looked at Cami and me. We smiled, and Cami said, "Just let us know if you need anything."

Brenda looked around. Then she walked across the arena toward Delilah. She was humming again. Her arms were not folded, but they were tight against the sides of her body. Delilah remained perfectly still. Cocoa once again stopped looking for pieces of hay and turned to watch Brenda. The pony's ears moved quickly, back and forth, and her eyes were wide. She blew out both nostrils twice. In some contexts, this could be a sign of distress and alertness in a horse. I leaned forward just a bit in case Cocoa decided Brenda was a threat because Delilah might get triggered into a defensive action. This behavior would be consistent with the way Delilah acted with other horses when she slipped into her dissociative fight mode. Fortunately, Cocoa decided Brenda was not a threat and relaxed her body.

Brenda stopped about 3 feet away from Delilah and started to hum a little louder. She gently swayed back and forth in rhythm with her humming. Delilah stayed still, her eyes locked on the woman for a few moments. Slowly, the gray mare stretched out her neck and moved her hooves four steps closer to Brenda as the woman reached out her arm in unison. They met at the same time. Brenda stroked Delilah's nose softly as she hummed, and the mare moved closer, bringing her head parallel to the woman's chest. Since Brenda was short in stature, Delilah had to lower her head past her natural resting place to align with the woman's heart.

Brenda swayed and sang to Delilah, then kneeled in the arena dust, continuing to hum and rock gently. Cocoa moved slowly toward the pair, her head and neck relaxed as she moved her lips and jaws in a licking and chewing fashion. For horses, this is generally a sign of acceptance and willingness to engage (photo 18). As Cocoa relaxed, so did I. The pony stopped about 10 feet away from the other pair.

Brenda sang to Delilah for a few more minutes, her hands gently stroking Delilah's mane and neck. Then she stood, turned, and started walking toward to the cone. Delilah moved freely with her. The rhythm of Brenda's singing never changed. Their footfalls matched each other as they traveled toward the cone. They passed the cone and Delilah and Brenda walked all the way to Cami and me. When she got to us we could see the same tear-streaked cheeks. There was something different from last week though. This time, Brenda had a smile on her face, and there was life behind her eyes. She appeared to be *present*, compared to the vacant look we had seen up until this moment.

We returned her smile. I asked, "Well it looks like you're here with us—and is that a smile?" My eyebrows lifted, and I waited, hoping she would direct the processing, thus taking control of her experience.

"I was still nervous. But I sang to her like I sing to myself or to my kids when things are bad. I think she was nervous, too. I think she knows what it is like when things are bad." She broke her smile for the first time. Her eyes welled with tears again, and they started to roll down her cheeks. "It was bad most of the time. I know I wasn't perfect. I know I neglected my kids… I would black out and stay in the bed for days, unable to take care of them. I couldn't protect them. I'm trying to do better now, but no one sees it."

She looked at Delilah, then Cocoa. "They see it, though. They know I will not hurt them, and I'm not going to leave them."

I glanced at Cami. We both knew I only had one question left before passing the baton to her for processing.

"What did the horses do that showed you they knew you were not going to hurt or leave them?" I asked.

Brenda turned to Delilah and started to hum again softly. Delilah breathed deeply; her belly expanded and retracted in a slow and steady rhythm that matched the cadence of Brenda's hum. Brenda ran her fingertips along the length of Delilah's neck a few times, then lifted her eyes as she caught Cocoa moving. The pony walked over to the gray mare, stopping next to her at a 45-degree angle off Delilah's left hip. Cocoa had joined them, but she stood so that Delilah was between her and Brenda.

Brenda spoke softly. "They are like me. They didn't know if they could trust me the first day. So none of us moved. I decided to try and move last week. So they moved a bit, too, but we still didn't know if we could trust each other. This week I decided to trust them, and they trusted me by moving with me." She looked at Cocoa. The corner of her mouth lifted into a little hook of a smile. "She still isn't too sure—she is curious, though!"

Cami asked, "Are you still a little unsure but curious, like Cocoa?"

"I am," Brenda admitted. "I really wanted to hate you guys and hate the horses. I don't think I can do that, though. I figured you guys would be like everyone else. But you haven't been. I'm not sure what to do now." She looked around the arena. He eyes stopped on a halter and lead rope that were hanging on the side of a post next to me. "What are those?"

I followed her gaze and reached out to touch them. "These are halters and lead ropes."

"What do you use them for?"

"Well, you can use them to help communicate to the horse where you want the horse to go. I guess you can say they are like a leash and collar for a dog. Sometimes they can be helpful, sometimes not," I said with a laugh.

"Are they scared of them?"

"It all depends. Both these horses were a little unsure at first with me, until they learned that I wasn't going to hurt them with either the halter or rope. But, like people who have been hurt in the past, I think horses always remember if someone hurt them. Sometimes they react to the halters and lead ropes just from habit. But if I slow down and remind them it is me, and I will not hurt or leave them—like you said a little bit ago—then they are okay again."

Brenda looked as if she wanted to reach out and touch the halters and lead ropes, but she didn't. "Okay," she said. "I was just curious."

Cami added, "Don't worry, you can ask us anything you have a question about. We might not have the answer every time but we can try to figure it out."

As Cami spoke the horses shifted. They both lowered their heads and shook their heads from side to side. Delilah reached down with her nose and scratched the inside of her right foreleg a couple of times, then yawned. After that, they both turned to walk over to the long side of the arena, leaving us alone with Brenda.

Cami and I both took the horses' cue to indicate the session was over. Brenda shifted her weight back and forth.

"Well, it looks like you got through the first activity of saying, 'Hi,' to the horses," I said, "and then the second activity of getting them to the cone and over to us. So next week we will move on to our next activity. Your homework for this week is to try and think of two possible treatment goals you would like to focus on for yourself while you are here. I know you had said in your intake that your main goal is to get your kids home. So maybe think about what two things you might need to work on to help make that happen." I waited a moment, then asked, "Do you have any questions?"

"No, I got it," Brenda replied. "I'll be here next week. Thank you." With that she walked over to the gate and looked at me, waiting for me to unlock it.

"Do you need me to get the gate for you?" I asked, remaining where I was.

"Oh, I didn't know I was allowed to open it." She looked sheepishly at the ground.

"No worries! It can be tricky to open and close, so sometimes I do it for clients. If you would like me to teach you the trick I can," I offered, now moving toward the gate.

"Ummm, sure…." Brenda appeared thrown off by my offer to teach her something. I caught the faint hint of a hum under her breath as I showed her how to open and close the gate latch. "Thanks. See you both next week," she said as she walked away.

Space to Share

Brenda was early again the following week, coming straight into the office and sitting in her usual seat. This time, she smiled openly at us both as Cami and I joined her.

I started the session. "So how was your week?"

"Okay. Are you going to ask me about my homework?" She leaned forward in her chair. There was an energy in her we hadn't seen before.

"Sure!" I replied with enthusiasm. "How did you do on your home—"

Brenda started talking before I could even finish the sentence.

"I need to learn to be proud of myself. I need to learn how to not be shut down." She went on to list all the ways she shut down. Brenda was aware that she dissociated, and in her own terms, "became a robot." She acknowledged that was how she had functioned the first couple of weeks at Unbridled Change because she thought we were going to judge her and not believe her story. She shared her long past history of abuse: being beaten so badly that she passed out and woke up the next day, bloody and in her own waste. She cried as she explained how her husband had told her children it was her fault, she was stupid, and she couldn't even keep herself clean. She unloaded and unloaded. Cami and I sat and listened. We held the space for her to say what she felt she needed to share.

Most of our 50 minutes that day was spent in the office. As it neared time to wrap up the session, I asked Brenda, "Do you want to greet the horses before you leave, or are you okay with waiting to see them next week?"

Brenda stood up from the table. "I need to say hi and pet them; otherwise they will not trust me."

This time Brenda didn't wait for me to lead the way. She opened the office door herself, only stopping and looking at me just before reaching for the gate latch to the arena. Although I was a little behind her, Cami was next to Brenda, so I said, "Go ahead on into the arena. I'm coming."

Brenda opened the latch, waiting and holding the gate open for me, then closing it behind us. She turned and went straight to Delilah. She stopped about 2 feet from the mare, letting Delilah close the gap and touch her first as she spoke to the horse in a hushed tone. She repeated the process with Cocoa. Then Brenda walked back over the gate, smiled at us and asked, "Can I go now?"

"Sure," Cami replied. "See you next week."

The following week she was annoyed with the way her case was going. Social Services didn't seem to believe her when she told them how well she was doing in our program.

We headed out to Delilah and Cocoa, where I started to say, "Okay, so today I would like you to—"

Brenda walked over to the halters and lead ropes, hanging near the gate. "I want to see if they will trust me like they trust you," she interrupted. "Can I go try to put one of these on them?"

I looked at Cami, and she shrugged, so I said, "Sure. As always, let us know if you need anything." Cami and I sat down on the side of the ramp to allow Brenda to have the full focus of the horses.

Brenda picked up Cocoa's halter first. The pony's halter had fun, multicolored bands of yellow, hot pink, green, and orange. The lead rope attached to it was blue. Brenda moved the halter around in her hands a couple of times, exploring it from different angles and holding different pieces of it. She made a decision about what she thought was her plan and headed off toward Delilah.

Delilah had been watching Brenda, too. She turned her head to the side and looked at the woman approaching her from the side of her eye, instead of looking directly at her, like she had in past weeks. Brenda caught the micro-change and stopped in her tracks. She turned and looked at Cami and me. I smiled but didn't move or say anything. I wanted this to be Brenda's show—not a lesson on how to halter a horse. I would wait for her to verbally ask for something before I would offer anything.

She looked back at Delilah. Delilah had turned to watch her now with both eyes. However, her body was still arched away from Brenda's direction. Brenda must have decided this was okay because she started walking toward the gray mare again, this time a little more slowly. Delilah turned and moved a couple of feet toward the other end of the arena, stopped, and looked over her shoulder at Brenda. Brenda stopped, too, and backed up a few steps. Brenda started to sway back and forth. She moved the halter around in her hands. After a few moments she turned and walked back to us.

"How is it going?" I asked with my eyebrows raised and a slight concern in my voice.

"She doesn't like this."

"What is she doing that tells you she doesn't like it?" I queried, looking at Delilah and then back to the halter in the blonde woman's hands.

"She walked away. She hasn't walked away before."

"You're right. This is the first time she walked away. What do you think that is about?"

"She's nervous." Brenda looked down at the halter and moved it around in her hands. "Maybe she doesn't know that I'm not going to hurt her."

Cami asked, "How can you help Delilah understand you don't want to hurt her with it? What do you want to do with the halter?"

"I want to talk to her...I want to put it on so she knows she can trust me."

"Okay," Cami went on, "maybe go try that now and see if it works. If not, come on back, and we can come up with another plan."

Brenda spent the next 20 minutes singing and talking to Delilah. The mare would come to her, then back away. Brenda would try to put the halter on. On some tries, she caught the webbed band over Delilah's nose...then it fell to the ground. Other times Delilah moved her face or hooves in the opposite direction, out of reach. Cami and I watched, noting any shifts or patterns in the client and horses. Whenever Brenda turned to look at us, we responded with different nonverbal body movements of encouragement, such as a thumbs up or a smile. She would smile back and return to trying to reach her goal of putting the colorful halter on the gray horse.

With only a little time left in the session I called out, "Just to let you know, you have about five minutes left today. No worries if you don't reach your goal...we can just pick up here next week."

Brenda nodded her head in acknowledgment but didn't stop working with Delilah. She had persuaded the mare to stand still again by singing and talking. Brenda used her free hand to stroke Delilah's neck, and the horse dropped her head lower into Brenda's chest as she had the previous session. Brenda inched the halter toward Delilah's nose. The mare sniffed the halter, then lowered her head a few more inches, dropping her nose in between two of the different colored bands of the halter. Brenda raised one hand higher, starting to pull a piece of the halter toward Delilah's ears. The mare shifted her weight but remained standing in the same place. We watched as one of the webbed bands got stuck on Delilah's nose and started to pull her top lip up, exposing her teeth. Brenda stopped immediately and relaxed the halter down a few inches, then considered all the different pieces before reaching out with her free hand to move the section of the halter that was getting stuck. This movement created a loop out of all the pieces that was now around Delilah's head. Brenda slid the loop over Delilah's ears and it fell down, encircling Delilah's neck. Brenda had created a collar out of the halter. In her hand she still held onto the middle of the blue lead rope.

She turned toward us, asking in a slightly loud voice so it would carry down to our end of the arena, "Is this right?"

I answered immediately, "Remember our saying, there is no right or wrong way of doing things out here because it isn't about horsemanship? As long as you aren't hurting yourself, the horse, or us, we are good with it if it works." I smiled, raising my shoulders and lifting my arms to ask, "So, does it work?"

Brenda looked back and forth from the halter hanging around Delilah's neck to me. "I guess. But now what?"

"Well, people use halters to take horses for walks." I hesitated to suggest she take Delilah for a walk because I didn't want to add another task to the day when she had already successfully accomplished a big one. So I just waited to see what she would offer.

"Okay." Brenda stood there, holding the rope, unsure of what to do next. Delilah shook her head and neck. Brenda took her movement as a signal of uncertainty, grasped the halter, and pulled it up Delilah's neck, over her ears, and off. She patted the mare's neck, talked to her, and walked back over to where we waited. Brenda placed the halter and lead rope back on the post.

"So tell us how it went out there today," I said.

"She let me get the halter on her. She didn't want it at first. I kept talking to her. She really likes it when I sing to her."

Cami asked, "What does the singing do for you?"

"I feel happy when I sing. So I thought that would help her, too. I didn't think she was going to let me do it, but she did."

Smiling, I added, "I didn't know if you would be willing to go through our program after our first meeting, but you are definitely showing us that you are here to work on your goals. Great job today!"

Brenda's face lit up with a huge smile of her own. "Any homework?"

I looked at Cami because I really didn't know where to go next with Brenda. Cami shrugged, so I asked, "What do *you* think would be good homework this week?"

"I don't know..." Brenda paused a moment. "Maybe to try and not be a robot and give people a chance?"

"Sounds like good homework to me!"

That day started a new pattern for Brenda. She came to our check-ins ready to share the week or pieces of her past story that she wanted to be heard. She expressed emotion and was present. In the arena she continued to work with Delilah and Cocoa. She always wanted to put the halter on first, even if she didn't use it.

Wiscy

Brenda had been in our program for a little over 10 weeks when she started asking about the other horses on the property. I explained that we moved clients around based on their treatment and relationship goals.

"Is there a different horse that you really want to work with?" I asked.

"I've been talking to the big black-and-white one over the fence. I think he really likes me."

I smiled at Brenda. "Well, that would be 'Wiscy,' short for 'Wisconsin,' where he's from," I said. "He is pretty, but he is also the baby on the property. He is only two and pretty full of himself at times. Right now we have clients work with him who want to learn how to hold stronger boundaries. Since he is basically a glorified toddler he can get pushy; he is still learning about personal space." I thought this new development could go one of two ways: really well so that Brenda could step into the next part of her journey to find her voice, or really badly, with Wiscy pushing into her space, which could be too much pressure (photo 19).

I knew Cami was thinking the same thing, but raised her arms up in the air and said, "Hey, it is up to Michelle which horse you work with!"

Brenda replied, "Well, I think I want to work with Wiscy. I can tell him no."

I thought for a moment. Brenda was having a hard time showing up other places as the confident person she was at the barn; she still fell back into her robotic facade with people outside the barn. Many of her "providers" had already categorized her and were not able to see the deep changes she was making. Brenda had been able to take responsibility for her part in having her children taken away. She was moving on in her personal life and starting to restore things that made her happy, like fishing and singing. So having the opportunity to hold her ground while still exhibiting caring and compassion seemed to fit with where she was in her treatment. Would Wiscy respect her? When we did open up more difficult subjects or hit greater challenges, Brenda still would withdraw, singing, humming, and swaying to reground herself and prevent herself from dissociating. Delilah and Cocoa would wait with her, remaining still. Wiscy, on the other hand, historically didn't like to stand still and wait for anything. He would become pushy with his enormous head and try to get you to interact with him (photo 20).

I had worked with Wiscy from the time he was five months old and built a strong relationship with him. Like all the horses I bring into a client session, I trusted and knew that if I needed to step in, Wiscy would listen to me and follow my lead, which would trump any interaction he was having with a client. In those brief seconds, with Brenda looking at me, I weighed the impact it would potentially have if I did not honor her request to work with Wiscy. She believed she was ready to hold a stronger boundary; she believed she was ready to trust in herself. She was asking for us to believe in her and to trust her, too. While she had asked for things in the past, this was the first time she asked for something outside of what we had already set up for her. It was a huge step and a potential turning point in her confidence and self-worth.

I decided to give it a chance, showing her that I honored and respected her request. We also came up with a plan "B": If it turned out that Wiscy was asking her to bring more energy and presence to the relationship then she could provide at this time, we would simply step back and pick a "middle-of-the-road" horse to help teach her the skills she needed to work with Wiscy again.

"Okay," I said. "Give me a minute to switch the horses around."

Brenda and Cami were already in the arena at the ramp when I let Wiscy in from the far end. He entered the ring with energy! His head was high in the air, and even though he was only two years old, he already stood a little over 15 hands. His long mane flowed up and down as he trotted around, looking every which way. Laughing, I said, "Well, you wanted him, so here he is!" I crossed the arena back to join Brenda and Cami at the ramp. Wiscy kept exploring, trotting from one gate to the next. He stopped long enough to look around, then threw in a neck roll and trotted off to check out another part of the arena.

I don't think Brenda knew quite what to do with his energy level. When she had been petting him over the fence line, he was always standing still, soaking up the attention. Now, in a shared space for the first time without a barrier between them, she could take in his true size and presence. There was nothing small about Wiscy. He could be overwhelming even to those used to larger horses. Honestly, a small piece of me hoped Brenda would change her mind, and I would implement my backup plan to introduce a horse with a more moderate energy level.

But no such luck.

Brenda asked, "Is he upset or nervous?"

"I don't think he is either," I answered. "He is used to playing in the arena with me, and he really likes to move around. Does he look upset or nervous to you?"

"I don't know. He is like my little boy who is always moving and getting into things." Then Brenda asked, "Will he stop running around?"

I smiled. Wiscy loved to run and play. I often joked the problem wasn't getting him moving, it was getting him to keep his hooves on the ground. "In theory, yes, if you ask him to and give him something else to focus on." My hope was that adding this hint of what to do next would help her determine whether she wanted to go out and try to connect with Wiscy or not. She had all the skills to do so from working with Delilah and Cocoa; it was really a matter of whether or not she was ready. I was curious to see if she would transfer those same relationship skills to a situation with a being that had higher energy and bigger movements. Brenda had not seen either of these things from the previous horses she had worked with.

Brenda accepted the new challenge. She picked up a brush and stepped a few feet into the arena. That was all Wiscy needed—he turned toward the woman and trotted straight up to her. Brenda had unknowingly called Wiscy to come to her using a cue I used when playing with the horses in larger areas (such as paddocks, fields, and even in the arena): When I stepped toward the horses and caught their attention with a whistle or hand movement, they learned I was asking them to turn and come to me. I loved that my horses could be "drawn back" to connection from my thoughts. It was exhilarating to see them perk up their ears and run toward me with friendly enthusiasm.

I don't think Brenda shared my enthusiasm for this trick, though. She seemed frozen. I shifted myself slightly so I was directly behind her just in case she needed help stopping the black-and-white gelding. Brenda knew how to stop a horse. She had practiced this skill in previous sessions. However, I was not sure she could access that information in the moment (photo 21).

With a slight question in my voice, I asked, "Brenda, do you remember how to get a horse to stop?"

Brenda's eyes were open wide. She appeared to be glued on watching Wiscy, coming straight at her with more energy then she had seen from the mares in our other sessions. She shook her head from side to side: "NO."

"All you need to do is put your arms up wide in front of you, and tell him to stop." I waited a couple seconds to see if she was going to respond. Wiscy was only a few strides away from her, about 24 feet, and closing. Keeping my voice flat on purpose, I asked, "Do you need anything from me?"

Brenda now nodded her head up and down in a yes motion. Her body did not move, even her breathing seemed to stop. I made the decision to intervene: Quickly stepping in front of her, holding my arms up in a "Y" shape, I said in a slow, low tone, "Whoa…stop…" A small cloud of blue stone dust came off the ground as Wiscy immediately planted his hooves and rocked back onto his haunches, stopping midstride. His head was high and his ears locked on me. You could see the muscling in Wiscy's chest tighten as he waited for the next cue he knew would come from me, telling him what we were going to do next.

I wanted to process what had happened with Brenda, and I didn't need Wiscy's play drive triggering her into a worsened state of dissociation. I decided to ask Wiscy to chill out and relax in a "ground tie" for a bit. I went up to the gelding and stroked his nose with the index finger on my right hand, telling him, "Good boy. Time to relax. Whoa—stand." I shifted my hand upward to make a stop motion, then added, "Stay…"

I turned and saw Brenda's face for the first time.

Getting Brenda Back

She was gone—the blank expression was back. Her breathing was shallow. Her arms were locked against her sides. It didn't feel like she was really looking at me or at Wiscy, who was behind me. "Brenda, are you in the arena with us?" I asked.

Brenda blinked a few times but no words came out of her mouth. It appeared that Brenda's flight/fight/freeze/faint reflex had been kicked into gear. She was operating out of the survival part of her brain. If we tried to engage Brenda in a discussion about her triggers at this point, we would not be successful and possibly even do harm, driving her further into freeze mode and possibly into faint. We needed to get Brenda back into the present moment so that both her mind and body would *know* that she was safe. Once her mind and body knew she was safe, then we could ask her mind to reach out to us as a familiar relationship and start to process what had triggered her.

So…Step One: Get Brenda present. Brenda had done better in the past sessions re-grounding to my voice. It is more authoritative than Cami's. Subconsciously, clients also know that I'm there to ensure physical safety and Cami is the emotional safety, so it naturally works for me to be the one that brings clients back into the here and now, while Cami takes over on the relationship level of the brain to process the "emotions" behind the trigger.

"Brenda," I said, "I need you to follow my voice and come back to the arena and tell us what you need. Cami and I are here. Wiscy is stopped and standing behind me." I used words that had worked in past sessions to reground her and "bring her back" to the present.

Brenda now turned her head and looked at me then Cami. Struggling for words, she said, "I don't know what I need."

Again, I relied on the regrounding sequence we had used in previous situations, a somatic method taught by author and psychologist Peter Levine, saying, "Okay. Let's do our body scan like we have done before and check in with our body to see if it knows what you need. That might help answer the question." I took a deep breath. "Let's start by taking a deep breath. It looks like you might be holding your breath, so let's go ahead and exhale. Good...nice and slow. Now, let's take three more deep breaths—in....out....in....out....nice and slow....in.... out.... When you are ready, let's start at your head and scan downward like we have before. What does your neck feel like?"

"Tight, like it is being squeezed."

"And your shoulders and back, how about them?"

"Stiff."

"Now your arms, what are they telling you they feel or need?" I watched as her arms moved up in front of her as I asked the question. Following Brenda's body movements gave us little hints and clues as to what she was feeling on the inside.

Brenda didn't seem aware that her arms had started to move. "They are stuck."

Since there was a discrepancy between her statement and what was actually happening in the physical world, I asked, "Can you look and see where your arms are right now?"

"They are..." Brenda stopped midsentence. Looking down, she noticed that her arms were not at her sides, but were, in fact, stretched out in front of her as if to brace for an impact or to push something away.

Wiscy gently nudged me with his nose and looked at Brenda. Historically, when I get a soft nudge from a horse during processing it means one of two things: Keep going, you are on the right track; or the client is getting anxious, so tread lightly. Over the years I have come to distinguish the signals. If a horse physically blocks me, cutting me off from seeing the client directly, then I know to back off and let the client process internally before moving forward because the client is getting anxious. At the least I need to acknowledge that we might be pushing our client's limits and give the therapeutic reason why I'm going to keep pushing so the client can choose how to proceed. I waited to see how Wiscy would guide me.

I remembered that I had put him in a ground tie. I needed to release him from the request so that he would feel free to give his input. I stroked his nose again twice and said, "Okay," my cues that he was allowed to move. Wiscy took one step closer to me but did not block me. I felt that meant I was on the right track. I looked at Cami; she nodded as well. So I kept going.

"Where are your arms and hands? What do you think they are trying to tell you?"

Brenda looked up at me, and to my surprise, I saw she had a faint smile on her face. She was on board and back in the moment. She knew what was happening. "My arms are up, trying to stop him! I guess I did know what I needed." She chuckled a bit and looked at Cami. She knew it was Cami's turn to ask the questions now that she was back with us and could safely dance between past traumas while staying grounded in the here and now in her mind.

On cue, Cami jumped in. "What else do your arms know?"

"They know that it doesn't always work. Sometimes I just couldn't stop him." Brenda was now talking about her ex-husband, not Wiscy. "No matter how I fought back, and you guys know I fought back like hell, I would still lose. The last time he beat me so bad my kids thought I was dead. He left me in the front yard like that…bloody, broken bones. I woke up the next day and I was naked."

Cami and Brenda spent some time unpacking that trauma and the timeline of that event. Then Cami asked, "What was different today? This time your arms moved, right? Did you lose today?"

Brenda looked at me, then pointed at me as she said, "No, because she stopped him. She helped me."

I let a warm smile come to my face as I softened my body, saying,

"I did help you. But *you asked* for me to help you. Do you remember asking me?"

Brenda shook her head. "No, I don't remember asking you anything."

"Well, you didn't use words. But your body asked. I asked if you remembered how to stop a horse. You shook your head no. Then I asked if you needed anything from me, and you shook your head yes! So your body totally knew what you needed and asked for help. I think that is pretty cool. And it seems to have worked. You got help."

"I guess…" Brenda didn't seem to know how to process the information that she had asked for help and that we thought she had done something right. Her eyes looked around the arena, searching for something.

This time Wiscy nudged me a little harder and stepped forward, closer to Brenda, but he still didn't block me. I took his cue and backed up a step. This movement brought Brenda's attention back to us, and she looked at me with wide eyes. Acknowledging Wiscy's proximity, I said, "Okay, now it's your turn. If you do not want Wiscy to come any closer or if you want him to move away, all you have to do is put your arms up and tell him to stop. Say, 'Whoa,' or 'No!' or any word that works for you."

As if on cue Wiscy started to walk toward Brenda again. This time, the blonde woman lifted her arms up and yelled, "NO! STOP!" at the top of her lungs. Her face flushed red and her arms trembled a bit. Wiscy stopped and waited, looking straight at her. With her arms still outstretched and shaking, a look of amazement came over her face and she said, "He stopped! He really stopped!"

"Yep, good job!" I smiled back at her. Wiscy turned and walked away, searching the ground for bit of hay. "Well, look at that…" I said as we watched. "I think he got your message."

Cami added, "So maybe your body is starting to have a voice? How do your throat and neck feel now?"

Brenda lowered her arms and turned to Cami. "Well, I guess they feel…they feel more relaxed, not as tight. I don't feel like someone is strangling me anymore."

"So, I want to ask," I began. "Do you want to try working with Wiscy again next week? Remember, no right or wrong out here…"

"I want to try him again," Brenda said firmly. "I like him. He just scares me a bit."

"Okay, so we have some homework then: journal about any thoughts or feelings that might come up as a result of today's session. You did a lot: requested to work with a new horse; agreed that working with Wiscy meant that you were going to need to bring stronger boundaries to the arena and be okay with working with higher energy than you do with the mares; and you asked for help when it was too much. Not only that, you were able to come back in the moment and realize that your body knew what it needed. You then tried it out, and it worked! All pretty big stuff. So, maybe in addition to reflecting in your journal, you can practice your body scan in order to bring 'you' back into your body if, at any time, you feel disconnected. As of today, we know your body is talking to you."

"He Knew I Was Hiding Something"

The next two times with Wiscy went well. Brenda improved her ability to tell him to stop. Brenda had plenty of opportunities to check in with her body and practice getting out of survival mode and into "relation-ship mode" with herself, Wiscy, and us. With each trigger she worked through unpacking past issues related to people being physical with her. In fact, Wiscy's sheer size was a trigger, but his respect and play drive helped her quickly recover and find what we called her "internal ladder of trust and respect" to come back to us. The ladder metaphor helps by giving clients both a visual and a language related to what their brain is doing with new information: running it through the three main parts of the brain, which deal with survival, relationships, and cognitive thinking.

Unfortunately, despite her hard work and progress, when Brenda appeared in court a few weeks later, it did not go well. Based on the recommendations of the social workers on her case, the court planned to remove Brenda's parental rights and have her children remain in foster care as their status changed to available for adoption. Brenda missed her first session with us after the court date. Cami called her and left a message saying that we hoped to see her the next week and reminding her we were here to be supportive to her as our client. We had already told her that regardless of funding sources—meaning the county paying for her sessions or not—we would see her if it was what she wanted.

Brenda came the following week and was early for her session. She came into the office, robotic again, which we expected: We knew she'd be either mad as hell or withdrawn and detached. Brenda methodically described the court's decision. She acknowledged that we had talked together beforehand about the fact that this was most likely going to be the outcome based on what we'd seen with previous visits with the social workers on the case. Still, Brenda felt it was extremely hard to sit there and hear them say that she "couldn't do the job."

She also said she was mad, but her body didn't show it.

Cami asked, "What do you need?"

"I want to go see Wiscy."

I hesitated because she did not appear to be in the room with us, and we had seen what could happen with Wiscy when she was actively struggling with dissociating. I agreed but began assembling a backup plan in my head.

Wiscy was on the far right side of the arena when we came in, drinking water out of the trough. We all entered the arena, and I closed the gate while Cami and Brenda went toward the ramp. Wiscy turned and walked straight, with a purpose, toward Brenda.

Brenda put a hand out. I think she meant to say hello to him, but I could tell there was nothing "in" the hello. She wasn't present. She was going through the motions of saying, "Stop," or "Hello," but it didn't matter which one she was intending—nothing in her body language confirmed that intent. Wiscy felt the same thing. He walked right into the woman as if she wasn't even there. His left shoulder smacked into her left shoulder, and Brenda fell stiffly backward, like a tree falling. There was no movement in her body to catch herself. Straight down, like a board, she went. I grabbed her right arm, but all I did was slow down her impact with the ground. Wiscy walked another 10 feet then stopped.

"Are you okay?" I asked as I helped her up.

"I'm fine." She let me assist her to her feet, then pushed my hand away. She didn't talk. She didn't brush herself off—the arena dust and pieces of hay stuck to her pants and shirt. She picked up a grooming brush and walked toward Wiscy. The big gelding let her get within 3 feet of him, then he walked away, turning down the long side of the arena. Brenda followed him, and the two walked in a stop-start pattern all the way to the other end of the ring. Cami and I were both torn about whether to intervene or not. Because Wiscy was keeping a 3-foot distance between him and Brenda, we agreed to let it play out for the time being.

Then the horse changed his behavior: He started to trot from one doorway to the other.

Our arena has four large, 20-foot-wide doorways with huge sliding doors. When the weather is nice, they are opened to allow in sunlight and encourage airflow. Two 12-foot pipe gates blocked the openings to the paddocks just outside the arena where our other horses napped and grazed. It was a cool, fall day, and the sun was out, so the doors were open. Wiscy was moving from one long side of the arena in a diagonal line to the large doorway on one short side of the arena, stopping at each of the closed gates and pushing against them with his body. It looked like he was trying to get out of the ring.

Humming, Brenda followed him from gate to gate.

Then Brenda sat down on the ground and started singing and playing with the brush in her hands. She had frequently sat down on the
ground when working with the mares Delilah and Cocoa, but they
respected boundaries and were careful with their feet. I wasn't con-
vinced Wiscy was an appropriate horse for a client to sit down around.
I looked at Brenda's position. She was against a wall with a large salt
lick box blocking one side of her legs. She wasn't completely vulnera-
ble. I decided to watch and wait, but I moved closer to her, just in case
I needed to intervene. I squared my body up to Wiscy—I wanted the
gelding to know I was there.

Wiscy continued to go from gate to gate; however, he added something new to the pattern: When he passed Brenda, he would stop, sniff
her arms and face, then move on to the gate before going back to her.
This went on for what seemed like forever. Cami and I kept glancing at
each other. We were looking for an opening to check in with Brenda,
but we did not want to interrupt the flow of body language between the
horse and our client.

Wiscy broke the pattern once again. On one of his trips past
Brenda, he sniffed her arms and then nudged her chest with his nose.
At first it appeared to be a light touch, then it looked as if he was push-
ing harder and harder. I grew concerned because Brenda was still sitting
cross-legged on the ground, and Wiscy's typical pattern of play was to
nudge things and then paw at them. I was not willing to let that occur
with Brenda. I started to move, but luckily, I didn't have to intervene.
Brenda stood up on her own accord and tried to walk toward me, where
I stood next to the gate in the middle of the long side of the arena. But
Wiscy blocked her and literally pushed her with his head, backing her
up. Thankfully, Brenda did not fall, but instead stepped backward with
him. I took the cue and slowly moved toward Cami, who was sitting on

the ramp. Brenda tried to walk toward the long side of the arena again. The gelding walked with her, then cut her off with his body next to the gate where I had just been standing.

Cami and I watched this dance continue. We could see that each time Wiscy stopped Brenda and backed her up, Brenda talked to him. Then he would turn and they would start walking again down the long side of the arena. After three or four stops and starts they reached the corner of the arena that had a large wooden mounting block, and Brenda sat down on it and kicked her dangling feet back and forth. She looked like a small child, struggling to speak and ask for what she needed. Wiscy was glued to her side, his massive head and neck over top of her, dwarfing her even further.

Brenda was crying. To us, this was a good sign because it meant she was feeling something. We waited.

"Did you see him?" she stated with emotion. "Did you see him? I don't know how he knew, but he knew..."

Cami asked quietly, "What did he know?"

Brenda reached down and pulled up the sleeves of her hooded jacket. There were two bandages, one around each wrist. Wiscy leaned his head down. With softness and care he gently sniffed both arms then blew his breath softly into her face, just as he had been the entire session. She leaned into him.

"I wasn't going to tell you guys. I wasn't going to talk about it." Brenda looked at us with the same pleading look she had given us when she first started at Unbridled Change. "He knew the minute I walked in today I was hiding something. That is why he knocked me down. That is why he would not let me brush him. He knew I wasn't to be trusted."

Brenda looked up at the gates where Wiscy had repeatedly leaned through the course of the session. "He knew I wanted to leave, so he tried to leave, too. Did you see him touching my arms? He knew what I had done."

Motioning at her own arms, Cami asked, "When did you do that?"

"Last week, after court. If they think I'm worth nothing I might as well be dead. They don't care, they took my kids…"

"Do you still feel that way?" Cami continued. "That you shouldn't be alive?"

"I did until a little bit ago." Brenda reached out and stroked Wiscy's face. "That is why he stopped going from gate to gate. I told him I didn't want to die anymore. Then he made me get up. He pushed me to get up."

"What changed?" asked Cami.

"I thought about my boyfriend. Do you know that I called my dad right after I did it and asked him to come help me? Can you believe that I asked for help from my dad? You guys have been telling me it's okay to ask for help for weeks, and I never really believed you. Now I do." Wiscy nudged her again. "I wasn't going to tell you guys any of this. That is why Wiscy kept stopping me. Every time I even thought I wasn't going to tell you he would stop me and take me back to the corner. Did you guys know that was what he was doing?" Brenda looked at us, waiting for us to give her some reassurance.

I replied, "I knew you guys were working something out, but I didn't know what. Now that you have shared with me what was happening, it all makes sense. Thank you for being willing to trust us."

Looking at the big black-and-white gelding, Brenda said, "I finally told him I would share it with you guys, and that was when he let me come over here."

Cami asked, "So, now what? Do you need or feel like you should to go to the hospital and get some help?"

"No," Brenda responded quickly. "I'm not going to try it again. I promised Wiscy. He knows it is true." Laughing for the first time in the session, she added, "Otherwise, there is no way he would have let me over here!"

"True…" Cami said. "So where do we go from here? Are you willing to look at what you have to live for now?"

Wiscy left and went in search for hay bits—once again the cue that Brenda was now ours, and we were free to process and help her determine where to go from here. Brenda said she knew that eventually her kids would be 18, so there still might be a chance to be a part of their lives. She understood that she could take initiative and write letters to them, sharing her love and desire to be their mom. She also recognized she had the ability to have more children, not to replace her children, but to expand her family and have another chance to be a mom.

Brenda thanked us and Wiscy, and she promised to follow the safety plan that she and Cami put into place for the week ahead.

Diesel Helps Brenda Graduate

Brenda stayed with Wiscy for another month, learning to set boundaries and also to play. She was learning to be willing to give herself the self-respect and power she had given to everyone else. Then one week she announced that she was ready to move on to the next part of her life: She wanted to marry her new boyfriend and start a family again.

"Wow, awesome!" I replied. "What would you like to do today, then?"

"I need to put a halter on Diesel," Brenda stated. She was standing up and looking out at Wiscy in the arena. She pointed at him. "He taught me it is okay to play and to say no. Now I need to prove it to Diesel!"

Brenda had first asked about Diesel shortly after starting with us at Unbridled Change. At that point, it was not possible for them to work together. Diesel had no ability to play nicely when he sensed a person was hiding something. It didn't matter what a person was hiding. To Diesel, it was a threat, and he was not willing to put up with negative energy. You didn't have to know how to "fix" what you were hiding, but you did need to claim it and acknowledge it. Because of this trait, Diesel was not a horse that our clients got to encounter in the arena until they had a couple skills—specifically awareness and acceptance. Cami described the process as "Name it, claim it, say it out loud, and then it loses its power." If a client wasn't willing to do these things when a limiting belief became clear, then Diesel responded quickly: He would pin his ears and remove himself, or if the threat was great enough in his eyes, Diesel removed the threat from his space. He had sent people running and jumping out of his arena or pasture with a glance or a charge.

But when a client could "name it and claim it," Diesel softened and became supportive. Clients had said they felt love coming from his eyes.

When Brenda first asked if she could work with Diesel, I had replied, "Well, eventually, yes, I think he would be a great one for you to work with. However," I'd gone on, "right now it would probably not be a good idea. Do you remember when I told you all our horses come from different backgrounds? Well, Diesel came from a mixed background of abusive training techniques and being a lone horse. The combination made him super-sensitive about when people are not being 'real.' If he thinks people aren't being real—matching their thoughts with their feelings, with their actions—then he isn't too nice about it. He requires a strong secure leader; otherwise, he is in charge. Sometimes that is good; sometimes that can be bad."

My explanation had the intended effect, and Brenda decided it was not the right time for her to work with Diesel.

I had completely forgotten about her desire to eventually work with Diesel until she pointed him out again during check-in that day. When I glanced at Cami, she shrugged, kicking the decision back into my court. Brenda had been doing amazing work naming and claiming her limiting beliefs. She was willing to see the "good, bad, and ugly" parts of herself. She had developed the ability to look at the "shadow side" of herself, as well. When the "shadow side" popped up in the arena or during the week outside our sessions, Brenda was able to catch it and show kindness to herself, instead of judgment. She understood that the "shadow side" was just the survival thoughts and behaviors stored in her subconscious, hanging out in the background until something triggered them. Brenda was now able to catch those behaviors in the moment, and instead of beating herself up or judging herself for them, bring a sense of compassion and understanding to why she was doing them and implement a new behavior or thought pattern in their place. She was now able to say no and set boundaries with higher energy—all things she would need to do to safely work with Diesel.

"Okay," I agreed, "but you realize that Diesel is much bigger then Wiscy? And do you remember my warning about him?"

Brenda looked me straight in the eye, and with a confidence I had not heard from her before stated, "Yes. If I can get the halter on him, I'm ready to graduate and move on."

I couldn't argue with her logic.

I switched out Wiscy for Diesel and then invited Brenda into the arena.

"This is Diesel." The big red dun horse was standing next to my right shoulder. His large 17.2-hand frame brought the top of his back even with my eyes—and since I'm 6'1" that is pretty tall! Brenda stood in front of Diesel. Her eyes were even with the middle of his chest (photo 22).

Brenda looked the horse over. His thick black mane flowed down his neck. He had his ears perked forward. He reached out his long neck, easily eating up the 3-foot distance between us and Brenda, sniffing her face. Brenda stepped back two steps into the arena wall.

"Well, he *is* big!" she admitted. And then, "But he's beautiful. He looks like a statue, not a live horse."

A proud smile crossed my face. "I'm kind of partial to him, myself,"

I said, "so I agree he is beautiful. Now, you said you want to get a halter on this big guy. Well, here he is, and there is his halter." I motioned with my head toward the large black halter, hanging off the wooden post next to the in-gate. "Let us know if you need anything." I gave Diesel another pat and ran my index finger along his silky nose to signal to him that I was breaking our connection and my role as his active leader—it was his time to connect with the client.

Brenda stood still for a couple minutes. She and Diesel just stared at each other. It looked like both were trying to size the other one up and decide what the next move should be. Diesel made up his mind. He walked over to his halter, reached out, grabbed it with his mouth, and walked out into the middle of the arena with it, shaking the halter in his mouth the whole time, like a dog with a toy. Brenda turned toward Cami and me with a stunned look on her face. I couldn't help laughing at Diesel's antics as I said, "Well, I did warn you he has opinions! If you want that halter, it looks like you will have to ask him for it." Diesel had stopped pretty much dead center in the arena and had turned to look at Brenda.

Brenda placed her hands on her hips. "Do you think he will let me have it?" she asked.

"I have no idea," I replied honestly. "But I do know one thing: Either you try and ask him for it, or you will never know."

Brenda accepted the challenge and started to walk out toward Diesel. The horse shook his head up and down, pieces of halter and lead rope tossed up into the air in every direction. Brenda reached him and appeared to be talking to him. We could catch only small bits of the woman's monologue, but it seemed to be something along the lines of, "Can I have that halter please? I want to put it on you."

Diesel replied by shaking his head from side to side in a "No" fashion. Brenda couldn't believe it. "He just told me NO!" she exclaimed. "He does have a little attitude, doesn't he?" Diesel pawed at the ground in response to Brenda and blew out a long breath. "Now what?" Brenda called to me.

Again, I smiled. "You asked for him. What do you think he needs from you to build the relationship to the point where he will let you put the halter on him?"

Every time Brenda reached for the halter Diesel would shake it enough to make her draw her hand back. After a few attempts Brenda shifted and changed her tactics. She moved to his side, out of range of the halter and lead rope, and started to hum. Cami and I smiled. She was grounding herself, unprompted and on her own. But in addition to the humming she was stroking Diesel's side with her right hand. Slowly Diesel started to lower his head and his tossing the halter around grew less violent. For the first time she was both grounding and actively being present and doing all at the same time. This might not seem like a big deal to some, but it was. It showed that Brenda was willing and able to systematically reassure herself that she was safe in the present moment, look to building and using the relationship part of her brain, and access the cognitive functioning part to problem-solve, all at the same time. We call that a full ladder of connection, linking flow in the moment from the lower survival brain, through the relationship part, and into the thinking part of the brain. This would have been nearly impossible for her when she first started her EPPC sessions. The flight/fight/fear part of her brain would have overridden any desire to stay present and work through the violent halter shaking and the sheer size of Diesel.

Diesel eventually dropped the halter and lowered his head. Brenda reached down and picked it up—now wet, muddy, and slimed with half-eaten hay from Diesel's mouth. She tried to loop the halter around Diesel's neck in the collar-and-leash style she had used with Delilah and Cocoa, but as the halter approached Diesel's eyes, he quickly popped his head straight up and sneezed directly into Brenda's face. The woman recoiled.

I held my breath, recalling all the times Brenda had shared instances when people spat on her. Somehow in the months she'd worked with the horses, not one had sneezed on her that I could recall (let alone doing it in the middle of her attempt to complete a task).

Brenda froze. She dropped the halter and lead rope. After a few moments, she reached up to wipe her face. Diesel lowered his head and sniffed her hand as she wiped the horse snot off. He let out short little puffs of air that moved her hair. Brenda didn't move away from him. Instead she reached forward and rubbed his nose. Diesel then lowered his head almost to the ground and closed his eyes. He shifted his weight, going from having all four legs equally loaded to cocking his left hind hip and dropping the weight of his left hind leg to rest just on the front toe part of his hoof. Brenda sat down on the ground next to his left front leg and stroked it as she hummed.

Later when we processed the session, Brenda told us she was telling Diesel all the things she wanted to let go of: all the mean things people had said; all the people who had hurt her. She knew that Diesel was going to keep her safe. "He didn't move one muscle," she said, "not until I stood up."

She was right. Diesel stood over Brenda for 15 minutes. His long black mane hung below his neck, brushing the top of her head. He looked like a sentinel guarding her. When Brenda stood up, Diesel raised his head slightly. The blonde woman reached down, picked up the halter, and slid it effortlessly over the big horse's head. Diesel and Brenda walked over to us together.

That was Brenda's last session.

What Came Next?

When Brenda finished her work with us at Unbridled Change, she felt she was ready to go out and try life! She did say she was going to always remember the horses and us.

"You believed in me and saw me when no one else did," she said to me. "How did you know I could be trusted?"

"I trusted my horses," I explained, "and they told me that you were hurt, and mad for sure, but hurt most of all. If my horses could trust you, then I could trust you. Trust is where we started, but you earned our respect. You did the hard work, week after week. Thank you for letting us be a part of your journey."

Brenda left with a smile and a presence. She did not get custody of her children, but what she did get back was herself. She walked out believing in her own worth, and she had *hope*, both for perhaps starting a new family, and for being there for her kids if and when they wanted to reconnect.

21. Brenda knew how to make a horse that was coming right at her, like this one coming at the camera, stop. She had learned it in previous sessions. But her first time with Wiscy triggered her old defenses.

22. For Brenda, learning to stand her ground and stay present in her body with a horse as large as Diesel—shown here with Michelle, who is over 6 feet tall—was quite an accomplishment. It filled her with pride and a sense of knowing that she was stronger than she gave herself credit for.

23. Like many ex-racehorses, Bear was a bit skittish, poised and ready to run at any moment.

24. Henry and Bally are grazing, moving in synchronous steps (entrainment), a sign of being at peace with me being in their space, although notice they both have an ear on me. Any sudden movement would certainly get their attention.

25. When another being embraces you with open love, the flow of compassion and understanding can transform hurt and pain into willingness. With an embrace like this one, Bear gave Gwen a gift that she would not receive from any human—an action that opened the doorway for her to heal.

26. The beauty and power of horses is mesmerizing. Hancock and Star, both senior horses and EPPC participants, share a moment that embodies horse exuberance at any age.

27. Horseplay can be rough, which is why Michelle was concerned about safe boundaries for Mason. Horses re-establishing social boundaries are not merely playing, they are confirming social order and what is acceptable behavior in a herd.

28. The herd ran up and down the fence line, kicking out, rearing up, and bucking. Mason wasn't afraid—he wanted to play with them!

29. Hooves, mouths, and lots of posturing show up in good-natured horse games, like King of the Mountain.

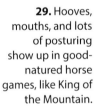

30. "How can you tell it is playing?" Michelle asked Mason. "Because, look! See, they aren't touching each other or hurting each other," he replied.

31. Horses adapt to the rhythm of footfalls, and when they are attuned to a companion, they walk in symmetry. That's what Jake's ponies did with him, indicating how well they understood his emotional and physiological state.

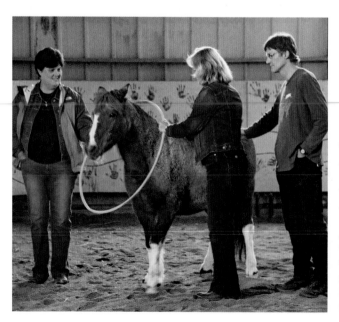

32. Jake used hula-hoops on the ground to symbolize his safe space. These workshop participants are using a hoop in much the same way— to inquire about safe space with the pony Puzzle. Just as Cookie and Squire gave Jake feedback through their body language, so is Puzzle doing here. What do you feel he might be saying?

33. Diesel turned around inside the box Ben had constructed and began to nudge one of the poles with his head….

34. …. One last hard whack knocked it over, and Diesel calmly walked out of the box.

35. Whether an American Quarter Horse racing the wind…

36. …or a Friesian Queen striking a pose, the horse's timeless beauty never fails to awe and inspire.

37. Traditional horsemanship is focused on tasks, and learning/conditioning your body to master postures in order to gain subtle, particular movements from your horse and yourself.

38. Horses desire to form balanced bonds and connections with their herdmates.

39. The horse is there to guide, give feedback, and provide a supportive partner that does not judge. At first hesitant, this young woman shows her delight when Miles curves around her to offer his head for connection.

40. Horses are willing to work through blocks, fears, and stumbles, and will stand with you, as long as your spirit is willingly engaged.

41. All creatures yearn for natural beauty and the freedom to live in peace and plenty. Through partnership with horses in EPPC, a doorway to a new story is created, one of healing and insight and unbridled change.

FOUR

Bear: I Will Not Leave You

Gwen

When I was working as the equine specialist for a residential treatment center that specialized in attachment therapy, I worked with one of the girls, "Gwen," for about a year. One session in particular was a turning point for her.

It was a spring day and Gwen made her way down the hillside toward the barn with her therapist. The girl had been having a rough couple of weeks. One would have thought she should have been happy: She was doing well at both the treatment center and at school. She was up for adoption and had met her "new family" numerous times. In fact, she had just come back for a long weekend stay with them, and they only had a few more home visits before she would be released from the residential facility for a trial placement as the adoption process finished out.

Exciting, Right?

Wrong! Gwen had been this far in the process a couple of times. Every time she would sabotage the placement, endangering herself or others. Basically, Gwen would come "off the rails" right before the adoption process was to be finalized and end up extending her stay with us or going back to detention.

Prior to that day's session, she had just come back from the home visit and immediately picked a physical fight with another resident, cussed out staff, and threatened to run away if they sent her back. Staff and her therapist tried to talk with her about what was happening and help her see the pattern of her behavior. But she was so volatile that day, no one felt safe approaching her.

Gwen was over 6 feet tall and built like a linebacker. When she became explosive, it was not uncommon for it to take three to four staff members to restrain her. She had once broken a hole through the sheetrock wall in an attempt to get to another resident in the safe room. It also wasn't uncommon for her to throw things and threaten staff and residents with her sheer size. Those at the residential facility learned to help reduce Gwen's stress levels by not pushing when she showed signs of accelerating. They found that the best place to process with her and hold her accountable was at the barn. With the horses, Gwen presented an entirely different persona. She was soft and almost small in her movements. She spent extra time helping with chores, and we could move her through her various triggers because she didn't want to hurt or scare the horses with her "normal" physical outbursts.

Learning to Trust Enough

Gwen's therapist had given me a heads-up about where Gwen was emotionally when they arrived that spring day. She wanted to try and plant the seed for Gwen to see the pattern of her behavior so that she could start to be aware of where it was coming from, because the feeling was that Gwen and the new adoptive family really were great for each other. The family was willing to work through Gwen's outbursts and wanted her to join their household.

During her sessions with me, Gwen had been working with Bear, an off-the-track Thoroughbred adopted from the Thoroughbred

Retirement Foundation. Bear was a large bay gelding, about 16.3 hands, and loved to run. Like many ex-racehorses, he was also a bit skittish, and clients had to learn to move more slowly around him than some of our other horses (photo 23).

The breeze was blowing, and I watched the clouds move slowly through the blue sky as Bear grazed beside me. We waited for Gwen and her therapist to cross the field into the grass arena where I stood with the Thoroughbred. As they approached, I smiled and asked my normal opening question, "How are we doing today?"

Gwen glared at me. "Fine."

Still smiling, I replied, "Well your body is telling me a different story, but for now we can stay with 'fine.'"

Gwen looked over at me with the corner of her eye and cracked a smile. "What are we going to do today?" she asked as she moved over to Bear and stroked him as he grazed.

"Well, I thought, given where you are at in working with the new family, it might be a good idea to explore how to show trust and respect again," I suggested. "A little bird told me that you do not want to go back to them." Gwen gave me a hard look. Holding my hands up in front of me, I added, "That's fine...I'm not here to talk you out of that choice. We are not going to worry about them right now but instead how *you* can show trust and respect."

"Okay, whatever..." Gwen grumbled. She dropped her hand from Bear's side and looked at her therapist and then at me.

I didn't want to give her too much time to build up resistance, so I said, "Great! You know how you and Bear have been working on him being willing to walk next to you?"

"Yes, he goes wherever I go. So what is new about that? He trusts me and will follow."

"You're right," I agreed. "He does trust you and follow you. He is showing you respect, too. But that is kind of easy for you guys now. I would like to see what happens when he is given the choice to listen and respect your requests, even if you are not right there next to him. This would show us how it might work when you actually do join your adoptive family for good. Will you keep making the right choices without all of us right there with you?" I paused. "So the activity today is to ask Bear to stay in one place that you choose and then see if you can walk away, do something else, and come back to him—with him still standing in the same place, hanging out, waiting for you. It's kind of like asking a dog to sit and stay. The horse shows he respects you enough to listen and trusts you enough to know that you are going to come back to him and not leave him forever. At the same time, you show him you can trust him enough to leave him, knowing he will still be there when you come back."

I looked at the therapist to see if she had anything to add, but she indicated we should go ahead. Gwen had been in enough EPPC sessions to know that my activity "directions" were typically vague and open-ended, leaving it up to her to figure out how to actually complete the task based on her own style and not mine. She also knew that we were willing to help her, but first she had to try herself and show she was making an effort to find a path or a solution. If she came to a place where she needed help, she could ask—but we would not do it for her. Instead, her therapist and I would help her break down the problem until she came up with a new idea to try.

Gwen approached Bear and asked him to pick up his head. He did. She then asked him to walk over to the middle of the ring. He did. She told him to stay, then turned instantly around and started to walk away. Bear stood for a second then walked off as well, put his head down, and started grazing again. Gwen didn't notice he had moved from his spot until she turned to check after walking about 20 feet away from the horse. Gwen huffed with frustration, marched over to Bear, reached down, placed her hand under his jaw bone, and picked his head up. She looked at him intently as she told him to stay again. This time Gwen didn't even get to turn and walk away before Bear took a few steps off the spot and returned to grazing.

Gwen turned to us, put her hands on her hips, and stated, "This is stupid. Bear doesn't care about me today. All he cares about is eating." Right after making the statement she turned back to Bear and yelled at him: "You stupid! Why are you ignoring me?"

The therapist reached out and touched my arm. She whispered that she wasn't sure if we should stop the activity and process what was happening, or maybe go to an easier activity. She feared that because Gwen had already had one altercation that morning the girl's fuse was fairly short. I looked at my horse. Bear was calmly grazing. He had an ear on Gwen but that was it. He wasn't showing any signs of distress, and he was choosing to graze close to her. I told the therapist what I was seeing and we agreed to let it play out.

Gwen stormed off and sat down on the mounting block in the middle of the grass ring, about 40 feet from where Bear was grazing. I'm not sure how many minutes she sat there—long enough for me to wonder if we should intervene after all. All of a sudden, Gwen exploded, yelling and screaming at the big bay horse. "You're so stupid! I hate you! I can't believe you are ignoring me, you motherfucker!" She picked up a small soccer cone and threw it at him.

My protector bristles went up—a rule of our sessions was you could not hurt yourself or the horses. I was about to call her over for a "time out" when I realized that Bear had not stopped grazing. Now Bear would typically startle and run away from anything sudden that moved around him, but here he was, head down, calmly grazing as a cone hurtled past his head (photo 24). Gwen's therapist was ready to pounce on her, as well, and I reached out and grabbed her arm, pulling her back to me.

"Look at Bear," I said quietly. "He doesn't care. He isn't running away. Let's see what happens. If he senses danger or a threat from her, he will let us know." Reluctantly, she agreed.

The cussing and screaming continued. "I hate you, you piece of shit! Why did I ever like you? Why aren't you paying attention to me! If you don't look at me I'm going to hurt you!"

Gwen got up and stomped around the ring. She came to a larger traffic cone and picked it up. Bear saw her movements, and his head came up, but he didn't move his feet. Gwen hurled the larger cone toward the horse. Bear moved two steps forward out of the way of the cone, and it whizzed past his rear end. He went back to grazing. This made Gwen furious. She screamed at him again to stop ignoring her. She picked up another cone and threw it. Again Bear moved out of its way and went back to grazing.

Something then shifted in Gwen: She went from yelling at the gelding to pay attention to her to yelling at him to keep away from her. "You better stay away from me! If you don't run away I'm going to hurt you! Did you hear me?" She looked for larger objects in the ring, next heaving a large plastic barrel toward Bear. The Thoroughbred's pattern shifted, as well. He stopped grazing and locked in on Gwen. His eyes, ears, and head remained totally focused on her. His body moved out of the way of the incoming barrel. When she went for another barrel, he moved out of its way, as well. But Bear wasn't moving away from Gwen. He was slowly closing the gap between them.

It was like watching a game of dodge ball. The enraged girl would find a random object and chuck it at him, yelling. Bear avoided the object and continued to approach her. By that point the things Gwen was screaming weren't even making sense. Mostly she was swearing at the top of her lungs. Bear made his move. He had managed to get within a few feet of her, and she had run out of things to throw. She was looking at him, still yelling, when the horse moved quickly to her, coming to a stop with his head over her shoulder and his chest against hers. I had a moment's concern he was going to knock her down and keep going, but he didn't. Gwen took her arms and shoved at Bear's chest, but the horse moved back into her. She shoved again with what looked like all her body weight. Bear simply moved back into her space.

What happened next I will never forget: Gwen started to cry. The tears were through the cussing at first, then they turned into overwhelming sobs. Her arms and hands locked around Bear's large neck, and she buried her face in his long mane. Gwen's whole body shuddered as she wept. Her knees must have given out because Bear slowly lowered his head toward the ground, guiding Gwen into a sitting position. Gwen kept her arms locked around the horse's neck, her face hidden under his mane (photo 25).

"He Didn't Leave Me"

Gwen's therapist went to move toward them, but I again held her back and whispered, "Bear has this. Let him finish what he started." She stepped back to my side. Bear had brought his head into Gwen's back and was, in essence, drawing her closer to him as she continued to sob with her whole body. Eventually, you could barely hear her crying and her body softened.

Bear lifted his head and neck and began to slowly back up, now lifting Gwen off the ground as her arms remained locked around his neck. We could now hear her talking to him, although we couldn't discern what she was saying. Girl and horse remained in the standing and hugging position for a few more minutes. Then, gently, Bear shook his neck and head. When he shook, Gwen dropped her arms and pulled away from him. She stroked his neck, talking to him.

Gwen stepped back from Bear, who remained locked on Gwen with his eyes and ears, facing her. The girl then held her hands out in front of her and motioned for him to stay as she stepped back a few feet farther. The Thoroughbred watched and didn't move a muscle. Gwen walked around him in a large circle. Bear didn't move his feet but followed her with his eyes and ears, and turning his head and neck to keep her in view.

After Gwen finished the circle, she walked back to Bear. She moved into him, again burying her head in his mane and hugging him with her arms. After a few moments she straightened her body, gave him a pat, and said, "Thank you."

Gwen turned and walked over to us with a smile. Her face was marked with tears and dirt. Wiping her face, she shared instantly, "He didn't leave me—no matter what I did, he didn't leave me."

I looked at Gwen's therapist and smiled.

What Came Next?

That spring day Bear showed us that trust comes in all forms. Afterward, Gwen was able to process with her therapist, discussing the trauma cycle she had acted out with Bear. Gwen then shared her story from the session with her adoptive family, and they assured her that they thought they could do the same thing Bear had done—they wouldn't leave her, no matter what.

Gwen was successfully placed in her new home, the adoption was finalized, and the last I knew, she was attending college.

Bear gave her what no human could. We all knew that Gwen needed to be held, to be felt, and to be seen by others, but she wouldn't let any of us do it. I believe Bear knew she needed him to not let go of her. Only Bear, a 1,200-pound horse, could give her what she needed.

FIVE

The Big-Boy Herd: Learning to Run and Play

Mason

Some of my favorite moments with horses are when I can simply watch as they gallop and play in their fields or paddocks. The beauty and power of horses is mesmerizing: tails up, nickering to their friends, playful tosses of their necks that send manes flying up into the air (photo 26). These moments are always joyous for me because I'm able to see the pure exuberance in them. The horses don't seem to have a care in the world but being in connection with each other. For most of the horses that I have worked with, the freedom, willingness to play, and ability to flow with connections—both with humans and other horses—is a significant change for them. Since most of our horses are rescues, many came malnourished, and in some cases, terrified of any type of contact. When I see them play and interact with others, especially within the freedom of the herd, I find myself very thankful to think of how much they have grown and healed their "broken" spirits. They have been able to find and embrace the "inner horse" that wants to run free and play in the field.

The parallels to the children and adults we work with are multiple. One client that always comes to mind when I see horses running and playing is a young eight-year-old boy named "Mason." He, too, had one of those histories that would make you sick to your stomach. He was a beautiful little boy, but he trusted no one. He had been in and out of different foster families since coming into the system at age five. His behaviors were so out of control that social services was considering placing him in a residential treatment facility. The foster care home where he was when he came to Unbridled Change had a real shot at turning into an adoption; however, Mason could turn on a dime from a sweet loving child to out of control and physically abusive to himself and others. The foster family had grown to love him but didn't feel safe with him.

Taking It Back

Mason showed his behaviors in the arena soon after beginning to work with us. He would be fine and open to the connection of the horses one moment, then turn to chase away the horses the next. Typically, the boy became aggressive when a horse gave even a hint of not doing exactly what he wanted. For example, if a horse dared to turn his back to Mason, the boy would throw objects at the horse. When horses were willing to work with him and were connected, Mason wouldn't let it last long. He would consistently do what we call "take it back." "Taking it back" is an action we have witnessed many times in clients over the years, especially those with attachment styles that are not secure. "Taking it back" tends to occur when a client begins to let walls down and show vulnerability to others—the subconscious brain kicks in and sounds the alarm: "Danger! Danger!" As a result of the danger alarm, the client picks a fight (frequently without conscious knowledge), often by asking for something completely inappropriate for that relationship or context. The result is the client "takes back" everything that may have contributed to building a relationship in a positive direction. For example, the client's brain can then say with total confidence, "See! He hates me! I'm better off on my own."

Mason would "take it back" almost instantly by physically pushing the horses or yelling at them. He would then turn to us, his treatment team, and state, "See, I told you they don't like me." Mason's brain had come to believe that any relationship meant "Danger, Danger!" However, I could see he also desperately wanted to be with people—he just didn't know how. It appeared he had decided that his safety depended upon a "my way or the highway" approach. If he made the rules, then he would know that he was safe. If you made the rules, he was going to get hurt.

Most of the time, clients with this attachment pattern chose smaller ponies or horses to work with. The interesting thing was that Mason was drawn to the bigger horses in the field. Almost every session he begged to work with the "big guys" out in the "big" field. I reminded him that we had stages for our clients, and they had to work their way up to the big guys. I asked him what it was that he liked about them. He stated that they were free and liked to play.

The word "free" is used constantly by the clients we work with, and the word is so telling. Even an eight-year-old intuitively knew that he was stuck in his thoughts and behavior patterns and not "free." Somewhere inside of him, he felt like a captive of his past. He shared that he didn't like being "mean" or "scary." When he talked to us about his actions, tears welled up, and he would say he didn't know why he did it.

"I just can't stop it."

We were starting to go in circles with him in the arena with his behaviors, as well, so I decided to give him a challenge. If he wanted to work with the bigger horses, he had to show me that he could put safety first. Many of the horses might walk away if Mason behaved inappropriately, but the big boys might not be so predictable (photo 27).

During one session I said, "Mason, you really want to work with the big horses, right?"

Mason nodded his head up and down over and over. "Yes! Are we going to work with them today?" He bounced up and down on his toes, he was so excited at the possibility of finally getting what he wanted.

"Well, here is the thing. Their legs are really long. You know how you get mad at the horses when they don't do what you want? What do they do?" I asked with my best investigating voice.

"They run away and swish their tail and get mad back," Mason said flatly. He knew my pattern well enough by now to realize that today he was not going to get what he wanted.

"That's right. Right now you have horses that don't really fight back. They just go away from you and don't let you get near them again until you are 'safe' again, right?" Mason nodded yes. "Well the big boys are a bit different. Their personalities are a bit more like you right now. If they get mad and someone is near them, it might not go over too well." I paused and waited for Mason to look back at me. "So in order for me to be willing to try a big guy with you, I need you to show me I can trust you not to pick a fight when you get mad. Because I really like you, and I don't think it would be good if you picked a fight and one of them fought back, right?"

Mason shifted his gaze from me to the large field behind me. Finally, he said, "Okay, that might not be the best idea. I might get hurt." Mason knew that while we liked it when he told us he was going to change a behavior, we always asked him to *show* us he meant what he said. We expected him to change his behavior first so then we could trust what he promised. "So what do I need to do to show you I'm safe?"

"It is pretty simple. I need you to try really hard this week not to pick a fight at home, and today during the session, I need you to not pick a fight with Starlight. If you can do that, I'm willing to see if one of the big guys wants to be your friend next time."

Mason agreed and shook my hand. We had a deal. We spent the session talking all about what not picking a fight would look like and "safety." We let Mason come up with a set of "rules" that helped illustrate what being safe would look like when he was mad. Starlight gave us plenty of opportunities to test Mason that session. The pony walked away from the little boy over and over. He even tried to grab a cone out of Mason's hand. We focused on studying the horse's body language and being aware of his own. When Mason started to react unsafely by yelling and trying to throw the cone at Starlight, we called a timeout and asked what he could change to create a safer situation. This had important parallels in his own life because he often made home and school unsafe because of his behaviors.

The Happy and Free Place

Mason didn't quite meet my challenge the first week. He had a couple of large outbursts at home. During the weeks that followed with the ponies, he came to the conclusion that he needed to build a "happy and free" place where he could go when he started to get mad. This would be a designated spot in the arena that he had constructed, where he could go to calm down and think about what he wanted to do next instead of simply reacting. He tried it out with Starlight and was excited to find that instead of Starlight running away from him, the pony joined him in his "happy and free place" after only a few moments.

The day finally came where Mason had held it together for an entire week. The little boy was so proud he was hardly able to contain himself during our check-in. I asked him which big guy he wanted to work with…and he picked the biggest horse we had: Diesel. The red dun gelding was still out in the large field where the other "big" horses and some of the younger rescue horses spent their turnout time. They were all the way on the far side of the 9-acre enclosure.

Mason decided he wanted to go and get Diesel out of the field on his own.

I was not so sure this was the wisest choice. "Okay, before you walk out there, what do you need to be safe?"

He stated, "Nothing, I got this!" Mason started walking toward the field. With some inner apprehension on my part, I decided to join him instead of verbally trying to troubleshoot his plan. To get to the big pasture we had to go through a smaller paddock that, at the time, didn't have anyone in it. Mason had learned that horses responded to his whistle, so he proceeded to whistle and call for Diesel before we even got to the gate of the big field. He got way more than he bargained for! All four horses in the pasture raised their heads, flicked their ears a couple of times, then took off at a dead gallop straight toward us.

I felt the urge to move the small boy back away from the fence and gate, but I was able to fight that instinct and wait it out. The horses closed in, galloping, bucking, and playing their way across the open field. I started working out a backup plan if they didn't stop at the fence! Diesel, for one, was totally capable of jumping out of the field, with his eventing background (he'd jumped plenty of solid fences in his day). I watched as the big gelding honed in on the fence, and me on the other side. It took all of my will power to wait and see what would happen next. Mason must have felt the energy from Diesel, too. He backed up on his own and moved behind me.

Game On

The herd still had about the length of a football field to cover to get to us when I glanced at Mason and saw he was smiling from ear to ear.

"Why are you smiling?" I asked.

He thought for a moment, then said, "I was a little scared, but I really want to stay and play with them."

"Okay...are you scared now?" I asked.

"No," the boy replied, "because you and the fence are here. That will keep me safe."

The horses arrived at the fence and took a hard turn, running up and down the fence line, kicking out, rearing up, and bucking with total abandon (photos 28, 29, 30).

"What do you think the horses are doing?" I asked. I was curious whether he read their behavior as play or fighting.

"They are playing with each other!" Mason replied with his smile growing even larger.

"How can you tell they are playing?"

"Because, look! See, they aren't touching each other or hurting each other." After a pause he asked, "Can I play with them?"

I wasn't sure where he was going with this question, so I replied, "If you are going to play with them, what do you need to do to stay safe?"

Without hesitating, he answered, "I need to stay on this side of the fence. See, I'm safe now, so it will be like my 'happy and free' place I made with Starlight."

I smiled and moved back from the fence line. "Sure," I said. "Go for it."

Mason had established his own rule for safety, and it was a good one. Game on!

For the next 10 minutes I watched as the little boy who was so unregulated when we first met found his own rhythm and rules of being in connection with other beings. Mason ran up and down the fence line with the horses, "playing" with them. If one of the horses reared, he mimicked the action, pawing his arms and hands in the air. He kicked out his legs in the same way the horses did when they bucked. When the boy finally settled down to a walk to catch his breath, so did all four horses on the other side of the fence. When he stopped, they came to a halt, as well.

Mason realized the herd was in sync with him. He asked them to follow, and they did. He experimented, taking off skipping and running, watching the horses match him on the opposite side of the fence line. Then he waited for one of the horses to move in some other way, and Mason followed and copied the actions. It was an amazing moment—not only was he enjoying the play, he was trying on the roles of both a leader and herd member. Mason was able to answer the horses' needs and wants as well as ask for and receive their feedback related to his own needs and wants. He didn't try and climb the fence or push the boundary of the rules he set for himself. He stayed safe. He was having fun! He was open to connection.

At the end of the session, Mason was so tired he collapsed on the grass and sat watching the horses through the fence rails. I gave him a few moments to just be with them. Then, when it was almost time for the session to come to an end, I asked, "What do you think that fence is like for you?"

He thought for a second, then said, naming his foster parents, "It's the rules Mom and Dad make. I don't like them but they help me stay safe."

"Hmmm, that's pretty cool. Anything else?"

Mason laughed. "You know, I thought I wanted to be on the other side. But you were right—the horses are too big! I think that wouldn't have worked out too well." He pointed at the fence. "That made it safe, and I still had fun and they liked me."

With a little smile I went on: "So are you telling me that you can have rules *and* be safe? If this side over here was the happy and free space, then you got to be happy *and* follow the rules?"

I winked and pushed my shoulder against his.

"I guess." He smiled and pushed me back.

What Came Next?

As we walked back to Mason's foster parents and therapist, waiting for us on the other side of the paddock fence line, I asked him to share the experience with them. They were so proud of him for making a safe choice. Mason was also proud of himself. At the next session, his foster mom and dad said they only had to remind him of the farm fence when he started to push boundaries and he had backed up on his own, taken a timeout, and then apologized. That day, that moment of play, was a turning point for eight-year-old Mason. Learning to see the world differently led to new pathways and connections in his brain and his spirit. I'm really happy to say he was adopted by his foster family.

SIX

Cookie and Squire:
Finding Your Voice
Jake

W hen we met "Jake" he was full of energy. He was excited about working with the horses, and he was extremely personable. He had good manners, smiled, and made eye contact. He was able to carry on a conversation during our intake session and share about his dog. Only when he talked about his dog did Cami and I catch a glimpse of sadness. He had recently been removed from his home and was having trouble with the transition—new foster home, a new school, and learning new rules.

Jake was referred to us because his grades were dropping, and he was starting to have behavior issues at the foster home and at school. His social worker thought our program could support him through the transition.

"I don't know what I think about not being at home," Jake told us. "I like the new house I'm in. It's fun, and the family is really nice. They bought me new clothes. But I still don't understand why I can't be back home. My grandma needs my help. It was my job to help her."

This was a loop that we heard over and over for the first few sessions. Jake was fixated on *why*. He was also fixated on not understanding *why*.

To him, his grandmother loved him. Sure, his dad couldn't be there all the time, but that meant he was supposed to be the "man of the house" and take care of things. Cami decided he might need more room to explore that question since it was one he kept coming back to during his check-in.

Building a Course

Jake worked with two of our ponies, Cookie and Squire, and they were all three drawn to each other. They often moved together throughout the sessions as a clump and looked like a "family" as they completed the various activities we gave Jake to build trust and respect with them. I thought the best way to help Cami reach her goal of giving Jake a chance to break down the *why* was to let him physically build what he thought had happened and what it felt like for him to move out of his home and into the foster home.

"Hi, Jake!" I greeted the boy and his caseworker, Sonya, when they arrived for the next session. In typical Jake style, he was beaming from ear to ear and ready to play with the horses. "How was school today?" I added.

"It was fine. I didn't get in trouble today like last week, so I think I'm ready to go play with my ponies now." He was already moving toward the arena gate where Cookie and Squire were waiting. Both of them had their heads up and ears perked toward Jake. "And see, they are ready to play, too! What are we doing today?"

Cami and I followed Jake over to the gate and let him in with his ponies.

"Well, you know how you have been asking us why you had to leave home? And how you don't understand why you can't go home?" I asked.

"Yep. Do you have the answer?" His response was full of the innocence of a child. Neither Cami nor I truly knew the *why*. We knew that his family meant well...that his mom was no longer around and his dad worked a job that required him to travel. His grandmother had tried to make it work but just couldn't meet his needs, and Jake was falling through the cracks.

Cami replied, "No, I'm sorry. We really don't know why either, but maybe we can figure it out today." Cami looked at me, and Jake followed her gaze.

"Okay, so you know how last week we made an obstacle course to take Cookie and Squire through to work on building their trust?" I said. "Well, I figured maybe we could do the same sort of thing this week. But instead of just picking four different obstacles, this week I thought maybe you could build a course that shows Cami and me what this whole process of moving from your old home to your new home looked like. Maybe if we build it and you walk us through what it was like for you, we can figure it out together."

Jake stood between Cookie and Squire, petting their necks as I talked. He remained still for a few moments after I finished describing the activity. You could see him thinking. He already knew I wasn't going to tell him how to build the course—that was up to him.

"Okay," he said, "so you just want me to show you what happened?"

"Yes, sir. And if you need anything, just let us know, and we will try to help if we can."

Cami and I backed up to the gate, where we joined the boy's social worker.

Over the next 15 minutes Jake built a massive course. He used pretty much the entire width and length of our outdoor arena—roughly 90 by120 feet. He also didn't just throw things together. He took his time building the physical representation of his world and what the process of being moved from his grandmother's home to a foster home looked like to him. First he laid poles on the ground in the shape of a house, pretty much in the center of the ring. He then put another pole off the house connecting it to a square, which he made out of four tires, one in each of the corners of the square. Coming off the square shape he put a series of cones, which turned the corner of the short end of the arena and came back up the long side. Down the length of the arena, about 120 feet, he took the time to make a few trips, gathering up armfuls of smaller toy props that he then threw down, spreading them out on the ground. His course then turned the corner at the far short side, where he placed three hula-hoops.

During Jake's building time, the ponies shifted to join us at the gate and turned to watch him. When Jake finished, he joined all of us as he announced, "So there it is. Do you want to know what it means?" He stood before us, resting his hands on his hips while he caught his breath.

"Sure, if you want to tell us now, that is fine," Cami replied.

"Okay." Jake didn't move to walk us through the course but instead pointed. "That pole box is my house, you know, where I used to live with my family. That single pole there, the one in the middle of the two boxes…" He paused to make sure we were looking in the right spot. "… that is for when I didn't know where they were taking me. The next box, the one with the tires, that's the new place I live. I don't really think of it as 'home' since I already have one, so I made it different. And those cones and all those other things on the ground are just all the other stuff I'm doing now. The hula hoops are me finally being back home."

With that he paused and looked back at us. I responded, "Wow, you put a lot of thought and time into building your course. How about you take Cookie and Squire through it now and share with them what all those different pieces are and what it was like for you in each part?"

Navigating the Course

Jake walked over to the pole house in the middle of the arena. He didn't ask the ponies to follow him verbally, but they did, without halters or lead ropes, one on each side of him. They walked in unison with him as he moved into the world he had created to share his story. Jake spoke softly, with Cookie and Squire moving in as close as they could to him. The ponies stood quietly next to the boy as he told them about his old home. We couldn't hear everything, but we did catch some: He shared that while he didn't have food and didn't really have a lot of toys or clothes, he knew it was home. He said he was sometimes scared in his home and didn't like being left alone. He turned and walked along the connecting pole that led to the tire box representing his new house. Once again the horses followed him, mirroring his movements (photo 31). They stood again on either side of him as he shared what it was like in his new house: He had food, his own room, and new stuff. But he was worried about his family and wondered if they worried about him.

Next, he turned to enter the "other stuff" portion of the course. It was like someone lit a firecracker under Cookie and Squire. The instant Jake neared the cones, both ponies stopped dead in their tracks, then literally ran in different directions away from the boy and the next part of the obstacle course he had constructed.

Jake had spent a lot of time catching the two ponies in the past. He had worked with Cookie for two weeks, just building up enough trust with him to convince the pony not to trot away and to instead stay and say hello to him. The sudden shift in the ponies' behavior didn't appear to throw Jake off at first. He simply remembered what he had learned in the previous weeks and spent the next several minutes trying to use that knowledge to bring Cookie and Squire back. However, after a few minutes, Jake's behavior also changed: he went from walking to running from one end of the arena to the other, as the ponies embraced a pattern of evasion, jumping over objects as they went. They'd pause, wait for Jake to get somewhat close to them, and then take off again to the opposite end of the ring.

Jake finally turned to Cami and me, and Sonya, and stated breathlessly, "I can't do this! They won't let me talk to them and show them!"

"I can see that you all are running around the arena right now, but it didn't start that way," I said. "At first it looked like you were able to talk to them and they were listening. What happened?"

Jake was taking deep breaths and leaning over. Throwing both of his hands up in the air, he pointed at the second part of the course and blurted, "They don't want to walk over there any more than I do!"

Cami followed up. "What do you need to be able to get through the next part of your course and to the hula hoops at the end?"

He thought about it, then answered, "I need help. I need someone I can trust to tell me the truth."

"Okay, who is that?" Cami asked. "What does help look like?"

He thought again and then pointed toward Sonya. "She can help me."

"Well, how about if you and Sonya go back out into the arena and work together to help the ponies come back and listen?" I suggested.

Jake turned to Sonya and stated with authority, "First, we have to get the trust of the ponies."

Finding "Safe"

By now, Cookie and Squire had split up. One was closer to us, and the other was down at the far end of the arena. Jake moved his body into a deep-thinking stance: He spread out his feet a bit and crossed his arms. He turned his head from pony to pony. "I think we should go up to Cookie first," he said to Sonya. "But remember, he likes to run away, so we need to move slowly and talk to him. He likes it when you talk to him. I think we should tell him what he is supposed to be doing. Cookie needs to calm down and listen to me as I tell him my story." He turned and looked at Sonya. "You ready?"

Sonya was a great sport, and even though she had not been out in the arena prior to this session, she answered, "Sure, but I don't know what I'm doing with the horses, so you will have to tell me."

"Okay, before when he ran away I had to let him know I was safe to be with," explained Jake. "So I think we need to build a safe place first for Cookie to come to, before we try to go through the part that was scary for him. Then he might be willing to go with us through the scary part to get to the safe place at the end." Jake pointed to the hula hoops at the end of the course, identifying them as "safe."

Jake approached Cookie, speaking in a reassuring voice. At first the pony shifted away. However, he did not immediately canter away as he had done before. Instead, Cookie walked a few feet, and then stopped and turned back toward Jake and Sonya. With the direction of Jake and the encouragement of Sonya, Cookie remained still and allowed them to approach and pat him. After a few moments Jake gestured for Cookie to follow them. "Come on, Cookie, you can come with us. We will keep you safe." The pony responded willingly, and Squire came over and fell in line behind Cookie.

Jake now had both ponies following him again. They went again from the home space in the center of the arena to the new house made of tires. They all moved together into the scary part of the course. No one ran away. Jake continued to tell both the ponies and Sonya all the things that he was worried about and scared about. Sonya embraced the moment and addressed the concerns Jake was sharing with her. The ponies stayed glued to Jake, once again looking like a family unit, moving together.

When they reached the hula hoops, Jake stopped. Sonya and the ponies stopped, too, and waited. They had arrived at the next safe place (photo 32).

What Came Next?

That session in the arena built a bridge for Jake. It allowed him a chance to walk through his story. But it also allowed him to *change* his story. In the middle of the chaos that came with the "scary" part of the obstacle course, he altered his approach. He stopped running and chasing after the ponies. He paused and asked for help. He took the lead and used his voice to tell his caseworker what he needed help with and asked her to support him. She responded and gave him assistance and answers. Jake was able to rejoin his family of horses and work through the scary part of his "life," eventually arriving at his designated safe place.

A new pattern emerged in which Jake could talk with Sonya about his fears in the moment. For the next few sessions at Unbridled Change, he explored his options, including trying to understand what his world might look like in the future. Jake asked questions: "Why do I have to stay in foster care? What does that mean? What would it mean to be adopted? What happens to my family if I'm adopted? Do I get to say if I like a new home or not?" Jake was learning to use his voice in a positive way to meet his needs, and the whole time Cookie and Squire stayed by his side. If they ran away, he would slow down, reset a safe place somewhere in the ring, regroup, and turn his attention back to completing the activity.

The impact on his "outside" life was significant: Sonya said all she had to do when Jake wanted to run or act out at home or at school was remind him of Cookie and Squire, and he would stop, regroup, and ask for help.

SEVEN

Diesel in the Box:
Trusting Yourself

Ben

Diesel's strong personality and powerful physical presence made him ideal for working with teenage clients who presented a "What's in it for me?" attitude. "Ben" had previously been through an anger management group therapy program with us before switching to our individual therapy program. Honestly, we didn't think Ben would last three weeks. He was gruff and had a hair trigger—he was always ready for a fight. He had been kicked out of the public school system for fighting, and he took pride in being able to take care of himself.

Cami and I noticed that underneath all the huffing and puffing was a leader. The other kids in the anger management group looked to him for direction. The horses looked to him, as well. The question always was, would he step into his role of leader for "good" or "bad"?

The group proved to be a place where Ben excelled. He stepped into his role as leader with care and a willingness to support the other group members. The group work allowed him a chance to see that his aggressive behaviors were not always working for him—after all, he had been in and out of detention multiple times and was on the verge of going back again if he violated his probation. During the 12-week course with us, he started to see that having support and asking for help were not such horrible alternatives to blacking out with rage.

Close to the end of the anger management group sessions, Ben asked us if he could keep working with the horses. When we queried what the horses did for him, he simply stated that they helped him believe in himself. The court system agreed and thought individual therapy work would help him address some of his negative behaviors and thought patterns on a deeper level. Because he had a fairly extensive history of being in and out of detention and countless different providers had tried pretty much everything to help him, the courts were willing to allow us the chance to be his next intervention.

Hard and Soft

Ben was an interesting mix of hard and soft. Most of the providers in his world (the court system, outreach specialists, social workers, school employees) liked him and were rooting for him. Ben knew that pretty much every professional in his circle was there to help him succeed. However, one day, he came barreling into the barn, blustering, "Everyone underestimates me, and they are just waiting to lock me up again! If they do, then they will see what happens."

It wasn't a good beginning.

Cami and I looked at each other and then to the probation officer who had brought him.

"Um, hi, Ben…. So it sounds like you are a little worked up. Do you want to take a moment and catch us up before we go into the arena?" I asked with some hesitation.

We spent a few minutes outside the arena to allow him space to "paint his picture." Then we heard the probation officer's version. The dialogue went back and forth, and Ben dug himself deeper and deeper into the "I'll show the world how bad I can get" attitude. Both Cami and I knew we were not going to convince Ben he might have options other than blowing up, beating the crap out of the next person who angered him, and getting sent back to detention.

Cami said, "Well, just remember you are the only one who can control what happens when you go back to court in a few months. You have a choice to make. You can turn back into the underestimated 'kid' you were when we first met you, mess things up again, and most likely get locked back up, or you can choose to keep growing and changing your behaviors, making the right choices, and go into court proving that you are changing. The choice is yours."

Ben shrugged and didn't say anything. Cami and I decided the check-in was over. I stood up from the table with the perfect activity in mind—"standing in the box." We entered the arena for the day's session.

"Standing in the box" was the same activity I had used with Gwen. I explained the idea to Ben: He was to ask Diesel to stay in one spot, but the horse needed to make the choice to stay on his own. Ben wasn't allowed to tie Diesel to anything. Once Ben thought Diesel was going to stay in one place, he needed to test the horse by moving away from him. Both Ben and Diesel needed to trust that Ben was going to come back and not leave Diesel alone forever, and that Diesel was going to respect Ben's request and follow the rules, even when Ben left the area.

After going through my overview of the exercise for the day, I said to Ben, "Remember, the focus of your task is to see if Diesel is willing to make a choice to stand where you ask him to, all on his own. There's nothing 'outside' of him that should force him to follow your rules if he doesn't want to. As you know, Diesel is an opinionated horse, just like you are an opinionated guy! For the last couple weeks you two have been figuring out how to give each other choices and respect. This exercise is the next step in building trust, respect, and willingness in your relationship."

The Jail Cell

Ben entered the arena angry and off-balance. However, as he got started, he seemed calmer and not quite as mad at the world. He noticed where Diesel was standing against the wall of the arena, licking a salt block. Right away Ben went to work, but he did not try to connect with Diesel first, as he typically did. Instead he began to move jump standards from the far end of the arena all the way over to where Diesel stood with his salt block. He moved other poles, as well, and started to literally "box in" the big horse. Ben moved the poles around and changed their spacing a bit. Diesel picked up his head and watched Ben from time to time, but then returned to licking.

Once Ben had the box the way he wanted it—with Diesel still inside, licking the salt block—the young man began to move away from the horse. Once Ben was a few steps away from the box, Diesel lifted his head, turned around inside the box, and began to nudge one of the poles. He knocked on the same pole multiple times, and it began to sway. Finally, the gelding gave the pole one last hard whack that knocked it over, and Diesel calmly walked out of the box, turning to look at Ben with a "Now what?" expression in his body (photos 33 and 34).

Ben took this as a challenge and said to us, "I think I need more poles." With that he walked back down to the other end of the arena to gather more equipment. Diesel stood still and watched Ben as the youth huffed and puffed and mumbled to himself as he tried to reinforce the box by adding more poles. Then Ben approached Diesel, going to his shoulder, petting him, and walked the horse back inside the box. Diesel followed his lead without hesitation.

However, before Ben could walk away, Diesel instantly knocked over a pole and again walked out of the box through the gap. Ben immediately tried to reinforce the structure, and Diesel continued to stand, wait, and watch. Ben, a little bit more frustrated this time, asked Diesel to follow him back into the box. Ben changed his approach this time, though: He sent Diesel through on his own and closed the box behind him. The problem was, the big gelding entered the box…and then kept right on going, through the poles and out the other side! Diesel would return to Ben on his own and stand next to the young man, waiting for him to "fix" the box. Over the next 45 minutes the pattern was repeated many times, until eventually, the horse decided to come stand by us instead of returning to Ben.

At this point the session was almost over; there was just enough time to do some processing.

"Ben, how about you turn around and look at what you've created today," I suggested. "What does it look like?"

Ben placed his hands on his hips and studied the structure he'd built again, this time from our vantage point.

"It's a jail cell!" he suddenly called out with a laugh. "Holy cow, I was locking Diesel up. No wonder he didn't want to stay in there."

"Okay," Cami responded. "Yes, it looks like a jail cell to us, too. Do you remember the directions Michelle gave you for this exercise?"

"Sure: to ask Diesel to stand somewhere still and wait for me to return to him," Ben said, still gazing at the jail cell.

"That's pretty close. Can you walk us through what your process was for coming up with the box you constructed?" Cami asked as a follow-up.

Ben answered, "Well, when I came in, Diesel was already standing over there, licking on that block. So I thought I could just box him in and then he would stay put while I walked around and came back to him. But the problem was, he kept breaking out."

I asked, "What would Diesel do each time he broke out?"

"He didn't do anything; he just stood there. He watched me as I made the walls stronger, then followed me in, and then he broke out again. I guess he got pissed at me—finally—and came over here to you guys for help." Ben finally turned and looked at us.

I smiled at him. "What do you think was going through Diesel's head while he was waiting and watching you build the jail cell stronger and stronger?"

Ben laughed and reached out to pat Diesel's neck. The big horse turned and nuzzled the young man's chest gently in return, grooming him back. "I don't know, he was probably wondering what the heck I was doing. I guess I just thought he needed something to get him to stay in one place."

Cami asked, "Do you need something to help you 'stay' in place and follow the rules?"

Ben laughed harder and even let out a little snort, "Uhhh, yeah! I don't do anything without being made to do it."

Cami followed with, "Well, how's that working for you?"

"Obviously, not so well if I built a jail cell for a horse." Ben smirked and looked back at his box.

I asked, "Do you think either you or Diesel need a jail cell to follow the rules?"

Ben shifted his weight and looked at Diesel, who had closed his eyes and was starting to fall asleep as Ben rhythmically stroked his neck. "I don't know. I guess I never even gave him a chance," the young man admitted. "I didn't think he would stay on his own. I saw him standing over there against the wall, and since he was distracted, I figured I could trick him into doing the activity before he figured it out and walked away." Ben paused and looked at the horse. "I didn't trust him…just like people don't trust me."

Softly I added, "What kept you from trusting him?"

"Nothing. He has always done what I asked him to do. I don't know why I didn't trust him." Ben voice trailed off at the end. We stood in silence for a bit. Then Ben spoke once again: "I guess it's because the only place I feel like I can trust myself is when I'm in jail. I know the rules, the people like me, and I can't mess up. I do better in jail then I do outside because in jail I'm not afraid I'll mess it up."

Cami waited a moment then asked, "Is jail your safe place?"

Ben instantly answered, "Absolutely. I don't have to worry about anything when I'm in jail, like my mom getting high or her boyfriend beating her up and then me beating him up. When I'm in jail, I get to relax, play video games, go to school, work out. It's a break from all the shit I deal with out here."

Looking back at the box, I added, "Hmmm, that might answer the question you had earlier. Diesel was totally willing to stand and watch you rebuild the jail cell and follow you back in over and over —all without resisting any of your requests. Maybe he was showing you what your pattern is."

Ben smiled and patted Diesel again. "Thanks, big guy, for showing me. But, man, that is messed up that you are willing to keep going back to jail." Ben laughed then, as he said, "I guess that is pretty messed up in me, too."

"Well, there is no right or wrong here, just information. But now that you see the pattern, is it one you want to keep repeating?" I asked.

"Hell, no! But how do I stop?"

"Well, like you said, Diesel stopped the pattern by walking away and coming to Cami and me for help." Cami and I smiled at each other, and I added, "If you had trusted him in the beginning, what would you have changed?"

Ben thought for a second. "I think I would have asked him to walk into the middle of the ring and stand there while I walked around the outside of the ring and came back to him. That would have shown him I trusted him, and he would have shown me he trusts me."

I replied, "Well, that sounds like a pretty good idea. I wonder if it would work?"

Ben looked at the middle of the ring. "I guess I underestimated him, just like everyone else has done with me. I didn't even give him a chance to prove he could do it. Just like people do with me, I assumed he'd screw it up and sent him straight to jail." Ben laughed again and shook his head. "Wow, you can't make this stuff up, can you?"

Cami laughed, as well. "Nope, we can't make this up. It is all you guys, playing out what you are dealing with in your lives."

Diesel Takes the Lead

Diesel woke up from his nap and created a massive bow shape with his neck as he stretched, then gently pushed on Ben's arm, moving him back a couple steps. This opened a space for Diesel to walk through. Diesel took a few strides forward toward the middle of the ring and stopped and looked back at Ben.

Ben looked at us. I laughed and said, "It looks like Diesel wants you to go with him."

Ben took the opening and joined the big gelding. Together they walked to the middle of the ring. Ben stopped and Diesel halted at his side. The young man put up his hands in a stop motion and asked Diesel to wait. Next, Ben backed up until he was against the wall of the arena. "Okay, big guy," he said calmly. "I'm going to walk around and I'll be back—wait…"

Ben walked all the way around the perimeter of the large arena. Diesel stood like a statue in the middle. The horse did follow the young man with his eyes and ears, but he didn't move his feet. When Ben reached the starting point of his lap, a huge smile broke out on his face, and he called Diesel to him. The gelding crossed the arena and the two of them met, Diesel lowering his head and letting Ben rub it. The two of them turned and walked back to us, side by side.

"Well, what do you think?" I asked as they approached.

Ben exclaimed, "He did it!"

Cami gave the boy his homework: "Yep, you both did. Now your job this week is to trust yourself. Next week we can dive more into what that jail cell does for you, but this week you can focus on the fact that you *can* do things without it."

What Came Next?

Ben came back the following week on a mission. He said he didn't want to check in for long. He wanted to give Diesel the chance to show he could be trusted again. So out we went to the arena, where Ben spent several minutes talking to Diesel and just walking around. Like the week before, Diesel followed Ben freely, stopped when he stopped, and walked when he walked. When Ben talked to Diesel, the horse would flick his ears and gaze at him. He was listening. Cami and I couldn't hear what Ben was saying; we didn't need to.

Ben turned to Diesel, held up his hands in a stop motion, and slowly started to walk backward away from the horse. Diesel started to move toward the boy, but Ben spoke again and moved his hands higher. Diesel took a step backward, squared up his legs, and watched. Ben walked small circles around the gelding. With each circle, Ben increased the size and distance between Diesel and himself. Pretty soon he was walking around the perimeter of the arena and Diesel once again stood like a statue in the middle, completely focused on Ben. His head and ears turned and moved with the young man, but his feet never moved. As each lap was completed, Ben's face brightened, his smile growing larger and larger. His body become more upright, and he appeared to step more confidently. Then, Ben went back to Diesel, and he stroked the horse's face and nose. He patted Diesel's neck and shoulder, once again talking to him. Ben turned and walked with the same body language over to Cami and me. Diesel followed along with him.

Cami and I smiled at him and asked him our typical opening question: "So how did it go?"

Grinning from ear to ear, he said, "It went great! Diesel just needed for me to believe he could do it on his own. Each time I made a circle I told him he was doing great and asked him to keep it up."

Ben eagerly talked about what it would mean for him to have someone believe in him like he had just believed in Diesel. He shared how it was a foreign concept to him. He had not even known what it might look like until the week before. He admitted that he thought he needed the breaks in jail to give him time to learn to trust himself again after he messed up.

What a realization! Detention and all the controlling mechanisms it implied was safer than home for him to build trust in himself. This insight became a turning point for Ben. It gave him an understanding of his own motivations and where his behaviors were coming from, as well as the new opportunity to build his own level of trust in himself outside of jail. Diesel asked him the same question we had: "Do you want to remain in the constant pattern of going in and out of jail or do you want to create a new relationship with yourself?"

Ben chose to start to trust and believe in himself.

EIGHT

It Takes a Herd
What We've Learned

In this book we have provided a glimpse into what EPPC sessions look and feel like, showing the power of enlisting horses as part of the equation in helping humans on their personal healing journeys. Like the clients you have met in the chapters you've read, typically clients of EPPC have never had contact with horses prior to starting their therapy sessions. Many only have abstract beliefs about what horses are, based on iconic imagery that portrays them as symbols of freedom, power, strength, grace, and beauty (photos 35 & 36). However, working with horses and their larger-than-life size and power in person provides clients with the opportunity to overcome any innate awe, caution—even fear—they may have related to horses. EPPC asks clients to move beyond their preconceived ideas about horses, and about themselves, to learn how to build a relationship with horses directly, in *real* life, with *real* feedback from another being. This is just one of several reasons EPPC works.

When clients engage in EPPC, they are also telling and retelling their story, which gives them a safe space for imagining a different story from the one that has kept them oppressed. At the same time, they are engaging with a transformative new story, solving old problems through the narrative agency of a new identity. When our clients face their fears through the assistance of horses, they begin to act and talk their way to a trust and self-respect they didn't know was possible in their situation. With all the client stories we've offered here, there is a common thread: *hope*. Many come to Unbridled Change feeling hopeless and overwhelmed by the process of working to heal past trauma. However, Equine-Partnered Psychotherapy and Coaching enables clients to find a safe haven with the horses and treatment team. The horses help build a bridge to embracing an amazing truth: namely, that our past does not have to permanently define us.

The Horse Cure proposes a process that can "make whole again," which is the very definition of *healing*. The reason EPPC is such a powerful intervention is that it sets the stage for people to see and work with all the pieces of themselves—mind, body, and spirit—in a quest for a sense of wholeness that overcomes the fragmentation of trauma. Traditional counseling historically focuses on the mind and now is expanding to include the science of our nervous system, as well as biofeedback to manipulate the nervous system. Traditional horsemanship focuses on tasks and learning/conditioning your body to master postures and positions in order to gain movements from your horse and yourself (photo 37). Traditional spiritual work focuses on quieting the mind and body to make room for enlightenment and for some individuals to transcend the physical realm. Each of these approaches in isolation has attempted to bring in more interactive and holistic exercises; however, they can only go so far because each is designed to only address *one part* of the person seeking help. What happens to the physical body takes up residence in the mind and the spirit. That's why the physical work of being with horses initiates a process that overrides the impact of physical and spiritual harm, and at the same time, begins constructing different thoughts and different spiritual responses.

Developing a real relationship and partnership with the horse creates a pathway for all clients to learn about themselves and then act to create the life they want.

A Healing Journey

The healing journey in EPPC starts the minute a client decides to change. It starts with rebuilding inner trust and then relearning how to trust others. Ashley had learned from her past that you couldn't trust anyone, including herself. Through working with Cocoa she had the opportunity to relearn and build new patterns. Brenda had learned to cope with emotional and physical abuse by dissociating and detaching from reality. Wiscy and Diesel opened a door for her to explore the idea that while she cannot control what others do or the actions they take, she *can* control her response and show up for her own life with purpose and hope.

From trust grows a willingness to start to address respect and self-worth. This progression sets the stage for the client to reclaim yet another piece of self that was harmed by trauma. Radar showed Ashley that he would respect her only if she was open to respecting herself and him at the same time. By nature, horses are the perfect nonjudgmental teachers when it comes to respect. They don't care about your social status or the other factors that usually figure into human assessments. Instead, horses care if you believe you are worthy of respect and ask for it consistently. Horses desire to form balanced bonds and connections with their herdmates (photo 38). As Sharon Wilsie, founder of Horse Speak˜, notes, the primary drive of horses is to preserve the safety of their space, and every communication is designed to establish, reinforce, or recreate a balanced space while also sustaining a healthy bond with others. Like humans, horses have to work at it, too, and especially because we humans are part of the equation. Horses will respect us as part of their herd, and even as a *leader* in their herd, when we offer clear communication and show respect in return.

Wiscy plowed through Brenda when she lost sight of her self-worth. She could not assert her own safe boundaries to affirm her own self-respect, and he showed her what that looked like. At the same time, Wiscy stayed with her, supported her, and showed her what she was feeling until she was able to ask for help from the treatment team.

Eight-year-old Mason explored how and why boundaries and rules are a good idea. Creatively enacting his relationship with the entire "big-boy herd" enabled him to identify behavior triggers in himself and choose a different path.

Gwen and Ben had both lost trust in themselves. Bear and Diesel showed them they were worthy of friendship and support by choosing to stand with them while they tried to figure out how to resume their quest for self-respect. The horses encouraged our clients to see the "obstacles" in their way and learn the skills of how to deal with them— either by asking for help, being open to support, or finding the courage to step into a new behavior pattern and try a new approach. Horses offer a remarkable opportunity for clients to embrace actions that can lead to healthy, sustainable, and sustaining relationships.

Not a Miracle

Like every intervention, Equine-Partnered Psychotherapy and Counseling isn't a miracle cure. The horses do not magically take away our pain, fears, and paralyzing "what ifs." The horses do not spiritually give us back our "soul" through mystical energy forces. What does happen is that a skilled team, made up of humans and horses, works together with clients to learn how to build relationships based on trust, respect, and willingness instead of force and manipulation. This approach sets the stage for clients to choose committed action to change their lives.

For us at Unbridled Change, EPPC is about empowerment, which means it functions as a step in the process of becoming stronger and more confident, especially in the context of controlling one's life and claiming one's rights. EPPC, by its nature, calls for clients to step into their own voice and power. The horse is there to guide, give feedback, and provide a supportive partner that does not judge people on what they look like, what clothing they wear, or what race, gender, or economic class they represent (photo 39). Instead, the horse makes judgments on how clients inhabit relationships, and how they treat themselves and others. When EPPC is set up effectively—with healing, mutually beneficial relationships and empowerment as the cornerstone—the horse has the ability to be a willing partner in relationship-building with the client, has an equal voice, and is not a tool or prop.

We are not suggesting EPPC can fix all woes or that it is appropriate for all humans and horses. We have had clients for whom this mode of therapy and healing was not a good fit and was not successful. It wasn't due to physical or mobility issues. EPPC can be thoughtfully adapted for a wide range of client needs. It is an emotional block that makes this mode of therapy not appropriate for everyone. If you are not ready to see the truth, to take ownership for your role in your *current* situation, and if you are not willing to change, EPPC will not work and may not be safe. Horses have no tolerance for "victim mindsets" or emotional dishonesty. To be successful in any therapy model, the client needs to be willing to change. A horse will stand with you as long as your spirit is willingly engaged and honest (photo 40). We feel it important to make this clear, because horse enthusiasts sometimes will overstate the potential of EPPC and obscure the rigorous work that goes into this model of therapy with mystical promises that falsify the process. In the end, we have found that horses are willing to walk through emotional hell and into greener pastures *with you*—however, you need to be willing to do your own work along the way, take responsibility for your own cure, and take the reins in your own healing journey.

The Right Horse

Just as not all humans are a good fit for EPPC, not all horses have the talent and personality to be a good fit as a co-therapist for human development. You will hear different opinions when it comes to this subject. Some enthusiasts argue that, by nature, any horse can do this work. Others will tell you that the horses themselves are "divine spirits" that heal the client. After working with many different horses, we disagree with both these positions. Horses are beings with their own personalities, talents, skills, and baggage, just like us. Just like us, they have things they like and things they don't. Just like us, their spirit can be broken. Just like us, they can love their "job" and have a purpose.

Horses must be carefully chosen for this work. Insisting that "any horse will do" is detrimental to the horse, the client, and the field. Therapy horses, like therapists, can be overwhelmed and experience burnout through repeated contact with toxic human emotions and energy. Skillful professionals in this field take care to give their horses the same mind, body, and soul balance they provide for themselves. Not every horse can step naturally into an empowered relationship. Just like humans, horses are affected by the actions of those around them. Understanding how animals—and in particular horses—think and feel positions us all to lead richer and more integrated lives. Animals are sentient creatures that we exploit at terrible risk, or embrace as welcome partners in our own efforts to become better human beings.

Horses are fully equal partners in Unbridled Change's EPPC practice, where we honor the dignity of the client and the dignity of the horse in a balanced dance of hope. Here's one final story that calls all the horses together, so to speak, and points toward our next project.

It Takes a Herd

"Nick" was a veteran. Tall, muscular, and broad-shouldered, his personality and attitude was over-the-top sarcastic. When we first met him, the energy that traveled in front of him was aggressive and explosive. It was as if he had a fortress of walls, traps, and land mines built around his emotional self, and nobody was going to get close to him. If Nick had come with a sign around his neck, it would have said, "Enter at your own risk, if you dare! I challenge you, bring it!"

Nick called and asked to set up a farm tour. He had heard about our program from a friend of a friend. His wife threatened to leave him if he didn't try to get help for his rage and suicidal ideations. He came into our office on a mission. I don't know if it was conscious or not, but the message seemed clear to us: "I'm here to try to shock you with my past, overwhelm you with my current issues, and get you to leave me alone and let me walk back out without signing up for your program."

In our office, Nick pulled out a chair, sat down, placed both hands interlocked on the table, and said in a gruff voice, "So what do you ladies think you can do to help me?" Before either Cami or I could respond, he leaned back, reached into his pocket, and pulled out a bullet. He placed the bullet on the table. "I'm going to use this to kill myself. Can you ladies give me a reason not to?"

Cami and I looked at each other. My thoughts raced through what our legal responsibilities were, then a sense of calm came over me, and I said, "I can't give you an answer that you will listen to. However, my opinion doesn't matter—the horses have the answer to that question. Let's go ask them."

I stood up and walked to the door. Cami smiled—she had been thinking the same thing. Talking to Nick at that moment was a waste of time and would be counterproductive. He was looking for a fight. We didn't want to give him one. Getting him up and doing something with the horses was going to be our best option and the best chance for him to choose to let us support him in his healing quest.

Nick looked confused, but he stood up and followed me. I didn't begin my normal intake talk about the barn rules and all of the other general information I usually share on a client's first day. Rules would just give this man something to push back against. We didn't have his trust and respect yet, so that approach would be walking into his minefield.

When we reached the middle of the arena, I looked in both directions and had to laugh. There, standing at the gates, was the entire Unbridled Change herd. They were lined up like sentinels, shoulder to shoulder. I could not recall any other time that the whole herd came together and stood at attention. They were alert, ears perked forward toward us, and completely still. It was not normal for all 10 to stand this way in silence.

Goosebumps worked their way up my back as I felt the horses' focus and energy on us. I had walked out of the office intending to let Nick walk through the herd and see which horses he was drawn to and which ones were drawn to him. I was now seeing that *every* horse had picked him! The message was clear: Every horse in the Unbridled Change herd was going to have a role to play in Nick's journey.

What does reactive attachment disorder and early trauma turn into when you are an adult? For Nick, those things equaled a deep sense that the world was not safe. He tended to attach quickly to the people around him. After attaching too quickly, relationships would hit a roadblock, and because the foundation of trust and respect was not there, they would implode. This pattern left Nick feeling hurt and disappointed by those he had trusted and given his loyalty to. Nick had a huge desire for love and family and a fierce loyalty to anyone he became attached to. He had an undercurrent of anger at the world for unfairly denying him loyal relationships in return for his dedication.

Nick's history included early childhood trauma and neglect, leading to foster care and abuse. He retreated to the army and was sent overseas where his already overactive toxic stress responses created the perfect storm in intense combat situations. When he came home, he was labeled with combat PTS and other mental health personality diagnoses. Explosive rage appeared with the littlest slight. His anger made keeping a job difficult. Because he felt he wasn't meeting the role requirements of a good husband and provider, his marriage struggled. His unpredictable behavior and his threats to hurt himself or someone else finally led to a last effort to find balance.

Nick shared this with us as we walked around, meeting each of the horses. We didn't ask for the information—he offered his story. It felt like he was placing a challenge on the table: *Let's see what you guys can do with this.*

"The VA [Veterans Affairs] wants me to take all these pills," he said. "I don't like what they do to me. They don't change anything. I still feel the same way. I just don't have any drive to do anything about it, so I guess they are working." Nick stood, petting two of our horses, Rafik and Otis. Rafik licked his hand and tried to nibble on his shirt. Nick broke into a smile and gently started to play back with him. This was the first movement any of the horses made as we worked our way around to each of the gates. It was also the first movement Nick made toward any of the horses. I was relieved to see them playing together; it gave me some direction. Rafik and his gelding group with Diesel and Otis were going to be up first.

"They Helped Me Find My Center Again"

Over the next two years, Nick built relationships with every horse in our herd. Some horses stood out more in his treatment, and some he built strong bonds with. Some of the horses you've met in this book became part of his story—Cookie, Squire, Diesel, Wiscy, Cocoa Puff, and Delilah—it took the whole herd. If you ask Nick, he will tell you, "The horses literally saved my life. I didn't want to live anymore. I had lost my purpose. I had lost faith in others, God, and myself. The horses gave me a chance to reconnect to all of those things. They helped me find my center again."

Nick's full story—how it took a herd—will have to wait for another book. My goal for this one was to open a doorway for you—the same doorway that our horses open every day for the clients who come to work with them. The doorway is one of healing, reflection, insight, and discovering that piece of "what's inside you" that you might have lost along life's journey. My dream is that through the stories I have shared you have experienced the power of the horse cure (photo 41).

About the Author and Photographer

Michelle Holling-Brooks

Michelle has over 20 years of experience working as an Equine Professional and Coach in the field of Equine-Assisted Activities and Therapy, specializing in working with clients to heal trauma, post-traumatic stress, and attachment issues. After a life-threatening illness at the age of 13 changed Michelle's life, a horse named Schedule A helped her heal her body, mind, and soul. Michelle is passionate about sharing the lessons

Michelle Holling-Brooks and Diesel

horses have taught her about healing and personal growth with her clients and other professionals. She believes that horses provide us all with the gift of awareness, the kindness of unconditional love, and an open challenge to us as humans to step into our own empowered voice.

Ann-Janine (AJ) Morey

AJ Morey is about to retire as an English professor and administrator at James Madison University in Harrisonburg, Virginia, and she has always loved horses. She has published books about the American dream, religion and sexuality, shaken baby syndrome, and vintage photographs of people and their dogs, as well as numerous academic articles on women's literature and religion and

Ann-Janine (AJ) Morey and Sophie

literature. After chemotherapy 15 years ago she found herself avoiding reading but completely fascinated by pictures. Rather than fighting this "brain change," she picked up a camera. She established Free Spirit Photography, LLC, in 2016, and she specializes in photographing equine-human interactions…and anything else that grabs her attention.

Unbridled Change

Unbridled Change is a non-profit organization located in Boones Mill, Virginia, nestled in the beautiful Blue Ridge mountains. In 2008, Michelle Holling-Brooks founded Unbridled Change with a simple but robust mission to provide high quality, outpatient, mental health counseling via Equine-Partnered Psychotherapy and Coaching™ (EPPC). Unbridled Change's mission also includes empowerment and life coaching, and training other professionals in the field of EPPC, as well.

Unbridled Change's main goal is to provide a safe place for clients to find hope, healing, and the growth they have been searching for. Through therapy and coaching services, clients are able to find the belief in their own power to handle life's ups and downs with unshakable confidence.

Unbridled Change works closely with various organizations that are also looking to support and help at-risk populations. These include school systems, foster-care systems, Juvenile and Domestic Relations Courts, private counselors, and private referrals from families.

One hundred percent of the author proceeds from this book go directly to Unbridled Change to help support scholarship and horse funds. To learn more about Unbridled Change, visit www.Unbridled-Change.org.

Appendix A
Resources on Equine-
Partnered Psychotherapy

Research and discussion about equines and equine-partnered therapies is a booming field in academic, horse, and mental health worlds.

Bowers, M. and MacDonald, P. (2001) The Effectiveness of Equine-Facilitated Psychotherapy with At-Risk Adolescents. *Journal of Psychology and Behavioral Sciences* 15: 62-76.

Brooks, S. (2006) "Animal-Assisted Psychotherapy and Equine-Assisted Psychotherapy." In N. Webb (Ed.) *Working with Traumatized Youth in Child Welfare.* New York: The Guildford Press, 2005.

Buzel, Alita A. *Beyond Words: The Healing Power of Horses. Bridging the Worlds of Equine Assisted Therapy and Psychotherapy.* Bloomington, IN: AuthorHouse, 2016.

Chandler, Cynthia K. *Animal Assisted Therapy In Counseling.* NY: Routledge, 2012.

Chardonnens, E. (2009) The Use of Animals as Co-Therapists on a Farm: The Child-Horse Bond in Person-Centred Equine-Assisted Psychotherapy. *Person Centred and Experimental Psychotherapies* 8 (4): 319-332.

Duncan, C. Randy, Steve Critchley, and Jim Marland. *"Can Praxis*: A Model of Equine Assisted Learning (EAL) for PTSD." *Canadian Military Journal* 4.2 (Spring 2014): 64-69.

Durham, Elena. "The Effect of Equine Assisted Therapy on Post War Veterans." *Emerging Practice CATS.* Paper 8. http://commons.pacificiu.edu/emerge/8. Accessed March 16, 2017.

Foden, Teresa and Connie Anderson. "Dogs, Horses and ASD: What Are Animal-Assisted Therapies?" https://iancommunity.org/cs/articles/asds_and_ animal_assisted_therapies. January 21, 2011. Accessed March 16, 2017.

Frewin, Karen and Brent Gardiner. "New Age or Old Sage? A Review of Equine Assisted Psychotherapy." *The Australian Journal of Counseling Psychology* 6 (2005): 13-17.

Klontz, Bradley T. et.al. "The Effectiveness of Equine-Assisted Experiential Therapy: Results of an Open Clinical Trial." *Society and Animals* 15 (2007): 257-267.

Hallberg, Leif. *Walking the Way of the Horse: Exploring the Power of the Horse-Human Relationship.* Bloomington, IN: iUniverse, 2008.

_____. *The Clinical Practice of Equine-Assisted Therapy: Including Horses in Human Healthcare.* Routledge, 2017.

Hamilton, Allan J. MD. *Zen Mind, Zen Horse: The Science and Spirituality of Working with Horses.* Forewords by Monty Roberts and Robert M. Miller, DVM. North Adams, MA: Storey Publishing, 2011.

Hayes, Tim. *Riding Home: The Power of Horses to Heal.* NY: St. Martin's Press, 2015.

Hempfling, Klaus Ferdinand. *Dancing with Horses: Communication By Body Language.* Trans. Kristina McCormack. North Pomfret, VT: Trafalgar Square, 1993.

Hanggi, Evelyn B. and J.F. Ingersoll. http://www.equineresearch.org/horse-articles. html. Accessed July 11, 2017.

Kemp, Kathleen et.al. (2014) "Equine facilitated therapy with children and adolescents who have been sexually abused: a program evaluation study." *Journal of Child and Family Studies* 23.3. 558.566.https://link.springer.com/ article/10.1007/s10826-013-9718-1. Accessed September 28, 2018.

Kendall, Elizabeth et.al. (2015). "A systematic review of the efficacy of equine assisted interventions on psychological outcomes." *European Journal of Psychotherapy and Counseling.* 15.1. 57-79. https://www.tandfonline.com/doi/abs/10.1 080/13642537.2014.996169. Accessed September 28, 2018.

Kirby, Meg. *An Introduction to Equine Assisted Counseling. Principles, Theory, and Practice of the Equine Psychotherapy Institute Model.* Bloomington: Balboa P, 2016.

Kohanov, Linda. *Riding Between Worlds: Expanding Our Potential Through the Way of the Horse.* Novato, CA: New World Library, 2003.

Knapp, Shannon. *More than a Mirror: Horses, Humans and Therapeutic Practices.* Forward by Linda Parelli. Ashville, NC: Horse Sense of the Carolinas, 2015.

Lac, Veronica. *Equine-Facilitated Psychotherapy and Learning. The Human-Equine Relational Development (HERD) Approach.* London and Cambridge, MA: Elsevier, 2017.

LeBlanc, Michel Antoine. *The Mind of the Horse: An Introduction to Equine Cognition.* Trans. Giselle Weiss.(2010). Cambridge, MA: Harvard University P, 2013.

Lee, Ping-Tzu, Emily Dakin and Merinda McLure (2015). "Narrative synthesis of equine-assisted psychotherapy literature: Current knowledge and future research directions." *Health and Social Care in the Community* 24.3. https://doi. org/10.1111/hsc.12201. Accessed September 28, 2018.

Lentini, Jennifer A. and Michele S. Knox. (2015). "Equine facilitated psychotherapy with children and adolescents: An update and literature review." *Journal of Creativity in Mental Health* 10.3. 278-305. https://www.tandfonline.com/doi/abs /10.1080/15401383.2015.1023916. Accessed September 28, 2018.

Mcullough, Leslie, Christina Risley-Curtiss and John Rorke. (2015) "Equine facilitated psychotherapy: a pilot study of the effect on posttraumatic stress symptoms in maltreated youth. *The Journal of Infant, Child, and Adolescent Therapy*.158-173. https://www.tandfonline.com/doi/abs/10.1080/15289168.2015 .1021658. Accessed September 28, 2018.

Johansen, Siv Grethe et. al. (2014) "Equine-assisted body and emotion oriented therapy designed for adolescents and adults not responding to mainstream treatment: a structured program. *Journal of Psychotherapy Integration 24*(4), 323-335. http://dx.doi.org/10.1037/a0038139. Accessed September 28, 2018.

Mandrell, Patti J. *Introduction to Equine-Assisted Psychotherapy. A Comprehensive Overview.* Np:np, 2006.

Mazzucchi, Ariana Strozzi. *Equine Guided Education: Horses Healing Humans Healing Earth.* Self. 2015.

Mueller, M.K. and L. McCullough. "Effects of Equine-Facilitated Psychotherapy on Post-Traumatic Stress Symptons in Youth." *Journal of Child and Family Studies* 26.4 (April 2017): 1164-1172.

No author. http://horsesandhumans.org/index.html Supports and reports research that will advance equine assisted therapies across all modalities. Accessed July 13, 2017.

No author. "Horses Help Heal Veterans' Invisible Wounds" November 1, 2014. http://video.nationalgeographic.com/video/news/141121-horse-therapy-veterans-vin. Accessed July 13, 2017.

Notgrass, Clayton G. and J. Douglas Pettinelli (2014). "Equine Assisted Psychotherapy: The Equine Assisted Growth and Learning Association's Model Overview of Equine Based Modalities." *Journal of Experiential Education* 38.2. 162-174. https://doi.org/10.1177/1053825914528472. Accessed September 28, 2018.

Nussen, Joy and Leslie Becker. *Soul Recovery: equine assisted activities for healing from abuse by others, loss of others and loss of self.* Redlands, CA: EquineWorks, Inc: Horses Reading People, 2012.

Parent, Ilka B. *Fundamentals of Equine Assisted Trauma Therapy. With Practical Examples from Working with Members of the Armed Forces.* Self, 2016.

Proops, Leane, Karen McComb and David Reby. "Cross-modal individual recognition in domestic horses (Equus caballus) extends to familiar humans." May 2012. http://rspb.royalsocietypublishing.org/content/early/2012/05/10/rspb.2012.0626. Accessed July 13, 2017.

Rosenberg, Shelley R. With Beck Andros. Foreword by Linda Kahanov. *My Horses, My Healers.* Bloomington, IN: AuthorHouse, 2006.

_____. *Accessing your Intuition.* Bloomington, IN: AuthorHouse, 2011.

Russell, Erin. "Horses as Healers for Veterans." CMAJ JAMC 2013 Oct 1; 185(14): 1205. https://www.ncbi.nlm.nih.gov/pmc/articles/PMC3787166/. Accessed July 13, 2017.

Schultz, Pamela N., G. Ann Remick-Barlow, and Leslie Robbins. "Equine Assisted Psychotherapy: A mental health promotion/intervention modality for children who have experienced intra-family violence." *Health and Social Care in the Community* 15.3 (2007): 265-271.

Signal, Tania; Taylor, Nik; Botros, Helena; Prentice, Kathryn and Lazarus, Kathryn. Whispering to horses: Childhood sexual abuse, depression and the efficacy of equine facilitated therapy [online]. *Sexual Abuse in Australia and New Zealand*, Vol. 5, No. 1, Jun 2013: 24-32. https://search.informit.com.au/documentSummary;dn=395058812631232;res=IELHEA. Accessed September 28, 2018.

Smith, Amy Victoria et. al. "Functionally relevant response to human facial expressions of emotion in the domestic horse (Equus caballus). *Biology Letters* 12.2 (2016). http://rsbl.royalsocietypublishing.org/content/12/2/20150907. Accessed February 21 2017.

Thomas, Lynn and Mark Lytle. With Brenda Dammann. *Transforming Therapy Through Horses: Case Stories Teaching the Eagala Model in Action.* Santaquin, UT: EAGALA, 2016.

Trotter, Kay Sudekum. *Harnessing the Power of Equine Assisted Counseling. Adding Animal Assisted Therapy to Your Practice.* NY: Routledge, 2012.

Trotter, Kay Sudekum et. al. "A Comparative Study of the Efficacy of Group Equine Assisted Counseling With At-Risk Children and Adolescents." *Journal of Creativity in Mental Health* 3.3 (2008): 254-284.

Williams, Tess. "Nebraska Veterans Turn to Horse Assisted Therapy." June 17, 2017. http://www.militarytimes.com/articles/nebraska-veterans-turn-to-horse-assisted-therapy. Accessed July 13, 2017.

Yorke, Jan et.al. (2012). "Equine assisted therapy and its impact on cortisol levels of children and horses: A pilot study and meta-analysis." *Early Childhood Development and Care* 183.7. pp. 874-894. https://www.tandfonline.com/doi/abs/10.1080/03004430.2012.693486. Accessed September 28, 2018.

Appendix B
Horsemanship Resources

These titles give a representative range of traditionally recognized horsemanship experts. Most materials about horsemanship are readily available on the internet and as video, and there are many new names that could be added to this list.

Brannaman, Buck with William Reynolds. *The Faraway Horses: The Adventures and Wisdom of One Of America's Most Renowned Horsemen.* Guilford, CT: Lyons P, 2001.

Dorrance, Tom. *True Unity: Willing Communication Between Horse and Human.* Word Dancer P, 1994.

Dorrance, Bill and Leslie Desmond. *True Horsemanship Through Feel.* Lyons P, 2001.

Hunt, Ray. *Think Harmony with Horses: an In-depth Study of Horse/Man Relationship.* Pioneer Publishing, 1978.

Jackson, Jaime. *The Natural Horse: Foundations for Natural Horsemanship.* Star-Ridge Publications, 1997.

Lyons, John. *The Making of the Perfect Horse. Communicating with Cues: The Rider's Guide to Training and Problem Solving.* Belvoir, 1998.

McCormick, Adele and Marlena McCormick. *Horse Sense and the Human Heart. What Horses Can Teach Us About Trust, Bonding, Creativity and Spirituality.* Health Communications, 1997.

Miller, Robert. *Natural Horsemanship Explained: From Heart to Hands.* Lyons P, 2007.

Moates, Tom. *Discovering Natural Horsemanship: A Beginner's Odessey.* Lyons P, 2006.

Parelli, Pat. *Natural Horse-Man-Ship: The Six Keys to a Natural Horse-Human Relationship: Attitude, Knowledge, Tools, Techniques, Time and Imagination.* Western Horseman, 2003.

Resnick, Carolyn. *Naked Liberty: Memoirs of My Childhood. Guided by Passion, Educated by Wild Horses. The Language of Movement, Communication, and Leadership Through The Way of Horses.* Los Olivos, CA: Amigo Publications, 2005.

Rashid, Mark. *Horses Never Lie: The Art of Passive Leadership.* 2nd rev. edition. Skyhorse Publishing: 2015.

_____. *A Good Horse is Never a Bad Color: Tales of Training Through Communication and Trust.* Skyhorse Publishing, 2011.

Roberts, Monty. *The Man Who Listens to Horses: The Story of a Real-Life Horse Whisperer.* NY: Ballantine, 1996.

Telllington-Jones, Linda. *The Ultimate Horse Behavior and Training Book: Enlightened and Revolutionary Solutions for the 21st Century.* Trafalgar Square Books, 2006.

Tellington-Jones, Linda and Sybil Taylor. *Getting in TTouch: Understand and Influence Your Horse's Personality.* Trafalgar Square Books, 1995.

Webb, Wyatt. *It's Not About the Horse. It's About Overcoming Fear and Self-Doubt.* Hay House: 2003.

Wilsie, Sharon and Gretchen Vogel. *Horse Speak: The Equine-Human Translation Guide.* North Pomfret, VT: Trafalgar Square Books, 2016.

Wilsie, Sharon. *Horses in Translation.* North Pomfret: VT: Trafalgar Square Books, 2018.

Bibliography

*These books and articles are mentioned in **The Horse Cure** or have directly informed our thinking about horses as sentient creatures.*

Bekoff, Marc. *The Emotional Lives of Animals. A Leading Scientist explores Animal Joy, Sorrow, and Empathy—and Why they Matter.* Foreword by Jane Goodall. New World Library: Novato, CA. 2007.

Braitman, Laurel. *Animal Madness: How Anxious Dogs, Compulsive Parrots, and Elephants in Recovery Help Us Understand Ourselves.* NY: Simon & Schuster, 2014.

De Waal, Frans. *Are We Smart Enough to Know How Smart Animals Are?* New York: W.W. Norton, 2016. ____

Goodall, Jane. *Through a Window: My Thirty Years with the Chimpanzees of Gombe.* (1990). With a new preface and new afterword. Boston: Mariner Books, 2000, 2010.

Gottschall, Jonathan. *The Storytelling Animal: How Stories Make Us Human.* New York: Mariner Books, 2012.

Griffin, Donald R. *Animal Minds.* Chicago: U of Chicago Press, 1992.

Grandin, Temple. *Animals Make Us Human: Creating the Best Life for Animals.* Boston: Houghton Mifflin Harcourt, 2009.

King, Barbara J. *How Animals Grieve.* Chicago: University of Chicago P, 2013.

Lents, Nathan H. *Not So Different: Finding Human Nature in Animals.* New York: Columbia UP, 2016.

Levine, Peter A. *In an Unspoken Voice: How the Body Releases Trauma and Restores Goodness.* Berkeley, CA: North Atlantic Books, 2010.

Low, Philip et.al. "The Cambridge Declaration on Consciousness." http://fcmcon-ference.org/img/CambridgeDeclarationOnConsciousness.pdf. Accessed July 14, 2017.

Morell, Virginia. *Animal Wise. The Thoughts and Emotions of our Fellow Creatures.* NY: Crown, 2013.

Morey, Ann-Janine. *Picturing Dogs, Seeing Ourselves: American Vintage Photographs.* University Park, PA: Penn State UP, 2014.

Morris, David J. *The Evil Hours: A Biography of Post-Traumatic Stress Disorder.* NY: Mariner Books, 2015.

Moss, Cynthia. *Elephant Memories. Thirteen Years in the Life of an Elephant Family.* With a new Afterword. Chicago: U of Chicago P, 2000.

O'Malley, Mary and Neale Donald Walsch. *What's in the Way is the Way: A Practical Guide for Waking up to Life*. Kirkland, WA: Awaken Publications, 2013.

Pollock, Mary Sanders. *Storytelling Apes: Primatology Narratives Past and Future*. University Park: Pennsylvania SUP, 2015.

Robles, Mario Ortiz. "Equids (might and right)". *Literature and Animal Studies*. New York: Routledge, 2016. 28-54.

Rudy, Kathy. *Loving Animals: Toward a New Animal Advocacy*. Minneapolis: University of Minnesota P, 2011.

Safina, Carl. *Beyond Words: What Animals Think and Feel*. New York: Picador, 2015.

Siegel, Daniel J. *Mind: A Journey to the Heart of Being Human*. NY: W.W. Norton, 2017.

Van Der Kolk, Bessel. *The Body Keeps the Score: Brain, Mind, and Body in the Healing of Trauma*. NY: Penguin, 2014.

Williams, Wendy. *The Horse: The Epic History of Our Noble Companion*. New York: Scientific America/Farrar, Straus and Giroux, 2015.

Wilsie, Sharon and Gretchen Vogel. *Horse Speak: The Equine-Human Translation Guide*. North Pomfret, VT: Trafalgar Square Books, 2016.

Wilsie, Sharon. *Horses in Translation*. North Pomfret: VT: Trafalgar Square Books, 2018.

Acknowledgments and Gratitude

From Michelle Holling-Brooks

I would like to start with the people that laid the foundation that allowed me to learn how to partner with horses: Mary Lou Glover was one of my main instructors at Junior Equitation School (JES), and she gave me the gift of a wonderful light touch with horses. She did not tolerate it if, as a rider, you hung on a horse's mouth, didn't hold your own weight, or had any other habit that forced your horse to work harder than you. Most of all, she emphasized that your horse's performance was directly related to the quality of your relationship with him. She was the first person to introduce me to the concept that if I wanted a solid performance from a horse I had to earn it by being *a respectful partner* with the horse. She taught me that if I *asked* a horse, rather than *telling* or *demanding* a horse to do something, the horse was typically more than willing to respond positively rather than picking a fight. She didn't believe it was the horse's "job" to perform—it was our responsibility to *create a desire in them* to perform.

In loving memory to Jane Dillon and Janet—you will always be in my heart every time I interact with a horse. Thank you for believing in a skinny beanpole of a kid.

Thank you to the friends who really tried to maintain a connection with me. A couple of them succeeded despite my best efforts to run them off, and I am eternally grateful for their steadfastness.

To my family, I am eternally grateful for the support and belief in our strength to find and believe in each other even in the mist of crazy chaos.

I want to acknowledge and thank Cami Murnane-Johnson. She is the "therapist" in most of the stories I shared in these pages. Partnering with her has enabled me to not only grow Unbridled Change, but her friendship and support has allowed me to heal and grow as a person, as well. She may not be the founder of Unbridled Change on paper, but I have always seen her as an equal partner in our venture and truly cannot imagine taking this journey with anyone else.

To AJ Morey: She has believed in me and supported me as I made clear my desire to write a series of books, sharing the lessons horses have taught me. She shares my passion to give back to this field and to help promote the role of partnership with horses in human growth and development. She has honored my voice, challenged me, and helped me form language around what is often unspoken—the dialogue between the horse and the client. Without AJ in my corner coaching me, supporting me, and taking the lead on gaining a publisher, these projects would not have happened!

To my husband: You have given me the safe place I never thought was possible in the human world. Without you and our daughters, I would not have been able to embrace the full teaching of the horses…that love is unconditional.

To all the clients, donors, mentors, teachers, and supporters that have walked this journey with me: I'm so grateful and humbled that you have allowed me to be a part of your sacred journey. You have taught me so much and thank you!

And to you the reader! Thank you for picking up this book and reading it. In doing so you are supporting Unbridled Change and our mission. One hundred percent of the author proceeds from this book go directly back to support scholarship and horse funds for this nonprofit organization.

From Both of Us

To Rebecca Didier, Martha Cook, Caroline Robbins, and the Trafalgar Square Books team: Thank you for helping us turn a dream of sharing the power of horses to help us heal ourselves into a reality. You walked us through the whole process of publishing a book with such kindness. Your editing, layout, marketing, and creativity helped turn this project into an amazing book that has the reach and power to change the lives of those who read it and the horses they partner with. Thank you doesn't quite seem to cover it! We are honored to join the ranks of TSB.

From Ann-Janine (AJ) Morey

Horse people communities come in different shapes. Mine has been the most loving imaginable, and so I am thanking my riding friends—Laura DeAngelo, Heather Kimberlain, Krista Suter, Debbie Young, Whitney Showalter, and Kay and Michael Walsh—for their laughter, wisdom, and encouragement as I have learned more about riding, horses, and photography. Additionally, I am grateful to Barbara Robbins of Rocky Hill Stables and Horse-Assisted Learning and TraumaHealing (HALT) and Jared Simmons of Simmons' Sport Horses for giving me access to take pictures, and for providing such good homes for me and my horses. Shelley Rosenberg of My Horses, My Healers Sanctuary graciously gave me photographic access to the International Horse Summit 2017 in Sonoita, Arizona.

Although I've never ridden with Michelle Holling-Brooks, she is a vital part of my horse life. She invited me into this horse-project relationship when I wasn't sure of my direction, validating my abilities as a writer and photographer, but also pushing me to grow. I am grateful she trusted me with her stories and very proud to have partnered with her on this book. She is a rare talent, and I'm fortunate to be part of her journey.

From the past, both distant and near, thank you to Pete Ferrell for putting me on Dobie and letting me think I was riding. I have a much better idea of how much work that little cowpony was doing with me aboard. And thank you to Shelley Aley for introducing me to her horses. I have a lovely memory of riding my mare Sophie with Shelley in the evening at Slate Lick and marveling at the fireflies dancing around us. Dianne Lowman, and Jimmy and Mary-Alice Walters offered caring support when I was having trouble finding the horses in my future.

My husband Todd Hedinger has been with me in so many ways. This brave man has cheerfully joined me on so many life transitions and horse adventures, and always with love and encouragement. If they are wise, men who live with horsewomen understand their place, but I'm here to assure Todd that it's an exalted one.

Finally, there is Sophie, named after Colonel Potter's horse in M.A.S.H. I commended Sophie to the rainbow bridge in August 2018, when she was too frail at age 35 to continue. She was my first horse, and I was fortunate to be owned by such a gentle, loving creature. Through her, I am acknowledging the healing spirit that horses bring to relationships with us, even when we don't always deserve it. The friendships named here have flourished because of the same horse spirit—steadfast even when we don't always deserve it.

Sophie

Index